MANCHESTER PUB GUIDE

The comprehensive guide to the city's pubs and bars

Featuring extended details of over 100 pubs and bars in Manchester city centre serving real ale plus listings for all other pubs and bars in the city centre.

Discover pubs beyond the city centre with special sections describing selected pubs in central Salford, Chorlton-cum-Hardy and Manchester's Wilmslow Road corridor.

Surveyed by members of the Campaign for Real Ale, the independent, voluntary, consumer organisation which campaigns for real ale, real pubs and consumer rights.

CAMPAIGN FOR REAL ALE

Published by the Campaign for Real Ale Ltd
230 Hatfield Road
St Albans
Hertfordshire AL1 4LW
www.camra.org.uk/books
© Campaign for Real Ale 2011

Map data © OpenStreetMap and contributors CC-BY-SA
www.openstreetmap.org

ISBN: 978-1-85249-302-8

A CIP catalogue record for this book is available from the British Library
Printed and bound in the United Kingdom by Delmar Press, Wall Lane, Nantwich, Cheshire, CW5 5LS

Edited by: Steve Smith
Designed by: John O'Donnell
Maps by: John O'Donnell and OpenStreetMap contributors

Production Team: Heather Airlie, Mark Charnley, Mark McConachie, Caroline O'Donnell, John O'Donnell, Rob Nicholson, Jane Spoors, and Roger Wilson.

Photography: Heather Airlie, Adam Bruderer, Mark Charnley, Chris Mercer, John O'Donnell, Andy Jenkinson, Derek Trillo.

Survey Team: Heather Airlie, Stuart Ballantyne, Ken Birch, Corin Bland, Adam Bruderer, Phil Booton, Peter Cash, Mark Charnley, John Clarke, Steve Davis, Andy Dickinson, Nick Earle, George Elmslie, Jim Flynn, Neil Furlong, Beverley Gobbett, Dave Hallows, Dave Hampshire, Tony Hayward, Andy Jenkinson, Mark McConachie, Margaret O'Brien, Caroline O'Donnell, John O'Donnell, Michelle Pratt, Jennie Ransome, Adrian Saunders, Laura Shiers, Steve Smith, John Sutcliffe, Steven Swain, Chris Wainwright and Karen Wainwright.

Front Cover: Andy Jenkinson with thanks to the Smithfield Hotel & Bar

Special thanks must go to the Waterhouse for allowing the use of their meeting rooms

Welcome to Manchester

Manchester is a vibrant city, steeped in history but not afraid to move with the times. From Roman beginnings through massive expansion as the heartland of the Industrial Revolution and into the present day, the city has grown and prospered.

It has many fine buildings, dominated by Alfred Waterhouse's masterpiece, Manchester Town Hall in Albert Square. Old buildings have been put to new uses - Britain's first passenger railway station, Liverpool Road, is now part of the Museum Of Science & Industry - but there are new buildings too, none less dramatic than the 168m high Beetham Tower that can be seen for miles around.

The city has a host of world class sporting venues including the two Old Trafford grounds (football and cricket), the Etihad Stadium, National centres for cycling, BMX and squash and one of Europe's largest indoor arenas with 21,000 seats for sport or concerts.

As a centre for business and learning, Manchester has arguably overtaken Birmingham as Britain's second city with office space in the city at a premium and the city's universities seeing unprecedented numbers of applications.

With all the visitors these many attractions bring to Manchester, it is thankful that the city has boasted a wide range of hostelries to slake the drinkers' thirst. From inns dating back to Victorian times to the most modern café bars, Manchester has it all. We at the Campaign for Real Ale (CAMRA) believe that pubs (in all their forms) have been part of the British way of life for centuries and should stay that way.

Recent years have seen a renaissance in the popularity of real ale and a host of new micro breweries open across the country and Manchester is no exception to this trend. Younger drinkers are sampling the new ales, enjoying the flavours on offer and making cask conditioned beer their drink of choice.

While all pubs have their place, we make no apology that those pubs and bars selling quality British ales are given prominence in this guide. We feature all pubs within Manchester's inner ring road and also take trips to Salford, the real ale packed suburb of Chorlton-cum-Hardy, and down the Wilmslow Road corridor.

Whether you seek a traditional pub with a roaring fire or embrace the café culture you will find it here. Join CAMRA in championing the real ales on offer and for now let's enjoy what's included here.

Contents

We hope you enjoy using this publication, but inevitably problems can sometimes occur. Should you have any cause for complaint regarding certain aspects within the pub then it is best to seek out a member of staff to put it right. If whatever matters cannot be put right, then you can contact local Trading Standards.

TSNW (Trading Standards North West) comprises the 22 Trading Standards services within the north west region of England. They can be contacted via their website (tsnw.org.uk).

You may also wish to contact the Councils which cover the areas within this publication. Their details are:

Manchester Trading Standards Service
1 Hammerstone Road, Gorton, Manchester, M18 8EQ
☎ 0161 234 1555
⊕ tradingstandards.gov.uk/manchester/

City of Salford Environmental Services
Turnpike House, 631 Eccles New Road, Salford, Manchester M50 1SW
☎ 0161 925 1346
⊕ salford.gov.uk

Inn Sight of Manchester's History

What is now known as Greater Manchester owes much of its expansion to being a major part of the industrial revolution. This is represented by some great engineering feats particularly involving transport. These include the Bridgewater Canal, the Liverpool and Manchester Railway and the Manchester Ship Canal. Each of these brought Manchester closer to, and to the attention of, the rest of the world. As would be expected, the rapid expansion during the Industrial Revolution led to a massive increase in population. The large number of people needed support facilities, not least of these being the public houses.

At the heart of this growth, the city centre of Manchester got its fair share of pubs. Over the years 'progress' has seen the loss of many of the city's original pubs, although thankfully some excellent examples remain. To compensate for this loss a lot of new pubs and bars have sprung up in former shops and new developments. As well as pubs the city is host to a variety of great and historically interesting buildings. Fortunately many of these can be seen close to some of our excellent real ale pubs.

Beginning on Liverpool Road across from the **Ox** is the '**MOSI**' (Museum Of Science & Industry – mosi.org.uk). This is built around the former Liverpool Road station, the original Manchester terminus of the Liverpool and Manchester Railway. The various galleries give an insight into the area's major contribution to the industrial revolution. The original entrance to the Georgian station is across the road from the **Commercial** although there is no access to the museum here. Adjacent to the main MOSI is the Air and Space Hall, formerly Lower Campfield Market, which houses a collection of aircraft including the designs of Manchester aircraft manufacturer Alliott Verdon Roe. His Avro company produced such famous aircraft as the Lancaster and Vulcan bombers. There is also a planetarium located here.

The area between the **Castlefield Hotel** and **Dukes 92** marks the terminus of the Bridgewater Canal. It is a warren of canal wharves, warehouses, brick arches and iron pillars. The waterways were a major commercial hub in their heyday and the main reason the Liverpool and Manchester Railway terminated here. The whole area is open for you to explore. The Castlefield Hotel overlooks the Staffordshire Basin which also

doubles as an events area. The Dukes 92 name comes from the adjacent Lock 92 also known as the Dukes Lock after the Duke of Bridgewater who had the canal built. This lock marks the junction with the Rochdale Canal which runs right through the city centre, a walk that provides respite from the busy city streets. The name Castlefield comes from the site of a Roman fort, Mamucium, built between the Rivers Irwell and Medlock and it was these rivers that allowed Castlefield to be the location for the canal basin.

The **Deansgate** is a next door neighbour to the **Beetham Tower** completed in 2006 and Manchester's tallest building. Its 47 storeys house the Hilton Hotel as well as private residences. Also the public bar, **Cloud 23**, on the 23rd floor offers marvellous and potentially vertigo inducing views across the city. Conversely the tower can be seen from all over the city and as such can be used as a way marker.

In Lincoln Square next to the **Rising Sun** is a statue of **Abraham Lincoln**. Lincoln had thanked the people of Manchester in recognition of their support of the Union cause. This support was given despite the Union blockade of Confederate cotton exports which led to the 'cotton famine' that caused great hardship in the Manchester area.

Next to the **Lost Dene** on Deansgate is the **John Rylands Library**. This impressive neo-gothic, red sandstone building belongs to the University of Manchester and is open to the public. It houses one of the world's finest collections of rare books and manuscripts but is worth a walk round in its own right. It was built by Enriqueta Rylands in honour of her late husband, a rich cotton merchant, and opened on 1st January 1900 (library.manchester.ac.uk).

Opposite the **Britons Protection** are the **Bridgewater Hall** and **Manchester Central** which are two important Manchester venues. The Bridgewater Hall sits on Barbirolli Square and is primarily, although not exclusively, a classical music venue. Manchester Central is built in the large and impressive train shed of the former Central railway station which closed in 1969. It was redeveloped and

reopened in 1986 as the G-Mex centre and became Manchester Central again in 2007. This provides a venue for contemporary music as well as trade and public exhibitions.

The **Lass O'Gowrie** and **Odder** sit across their respective roads from New Broadcasting House, the former home of **BBC** Manchester, now superseded by Media City in Salford Quays. Opened in 1975 to replace the smaller facilities in Piccadilly, it was home to many notable productions including 'A Question of Sport', 'Mastermind', 'Life on Mars' and 'It's a Knockout', as well as numerous radio programmes. At time of publishing, the site has been sold to local developer, Reality Estates, and redevelopment beckons.

Next door but one to **Fab Café** is **CUBE** (Centre for the Urban Built Environment – cube.org.uk); this is the city's gallery for architecture and the built environment. It hosts regular exhibitions featuring mostly photography and architectural models.

The area between the **Seven Oaks, Grey Horse, Circus Tavern** and the **Old Monkey** is the location of Manchester's **China Town**. This enclave is full of Chinese restaurants and shops and sustains a thriving Chinese community. The current area itself has its origins in the 1970s although a Chinese community existed in the city before this. The **Imperial Chinese**

Arch on Faulkner Street was erected in 1987 and is adorned with symbols of luck and prosperity. The Chinese New Year is a time of major celebration and the annual parade attracts thousands of people. Across the road from the Seven Oaks is **Manchester Art Gallery** (manchestergalleries.org). The gallery is a complex of three buildings with its main entrance on Mosley Street. With twenty one rooms and over two thousand items on display at any one time make sure you give yourself plenty of time to look around.

Sitting outside the **Waterhouse** you can gaze upon Manchester **Town Hall** which is widely regarded as the city's finest building. On the hour you can also listen to 'Great Abel' the large hour bell in the clock tower which can be heard all over the city. Designed in Gothic style by Alfred Waterhouse (hence the name of the pub) it was built between 1868 and 1877 to replace the original, much smaller town hall on King Street. It consists of fourteen million bricks encased in Spinkwell stone. To the left of this is St. Peter's Square which was the site of the eponymous church demolished in 1907. It is currently home to a Cenotaph erected after the First World War and a Metrolink stop.

Manchester's well established **Gay Village** is home to an improving selection of pubs selling real ale. The long established hostelries, including **Paddys Goose,** the **Eagle** and the **Rembrant** have been joined by the **Molly House** and **Eden**. The village itself is centred on Canal Street by the Rochdale Canal and began to take off in the early nineties. Some bars in the area had attracted a gay and lesbian clientele long before this, although it could almost have been described as an underground movement. However, the City Council began to introduce non-discriminatory policies at the same time as the Central Manchester Development Corporation started to improve what had become a run down area. This led to some entrepreneurs effectively coming out into the open and providing venues where people did not have to fear intimidation because of their sexuality. Their success is demonstrated by the huge Gay Pride festival held annually and attended by people from all over the world.

The **Bank** on Mosley Street lies beneath the Portico Library and Gallery (theportico.org.uk) which is accessed from Charlotte Street round the corner. Opened in 1806 by Manchester businessmen who wanted to combine the uses of a newsroom and a library, it is a fine example of Neo-Classical architecture designed by Thomas Harrison with a fine glass and plaster dome providing illumination of the gallery.

At one corner of Piccadilly Gardens, regarded as the heart of the city, **Wetherspoons (Manchester & County)** faces the statue of the Duke of Wellington. Behind him is the relatively new 'One Piccadilly Gardens' built in 2003 as part of a much needed revamp of the area. Opinion on this building is divided but it does contain **Kro Piccadilly** where you can enjoy a pint and look across the gardens to the fountain (when it's turned on) and statues of Queen Victoria, James Watt and Sir Robert Peel.

Inn Sight of Manchester's History

Lloyds No 1 (Seven Stars) is a part of the **Printworks** complex. Originally built in 1873 as Withy Grove Printing House it later became known as Kemsley House, Thompson House and for a while Maxwell House. This was latterly the home of the Daily Mirror newspaper amongst others until closure in 1985. Its redevelopment was spurred on by the 1996 IRA bomb attack and reopened in 2000. It is now home to a cinema and a variety of bars and eateries.

The **MicroBar** is part of the Arndale Market food hall and provides a welcome break from the rigours of shopping. You can enjoy a beer from the bar and food from any of the surrounding food outlets. The massive **Arndale Centre** complex was completed in 1980 and is a monument to retail therapy. Part of it was redeveloped after the 1996 bombing, a recurring theme in this part of the city. The Arndale Market was itself redeveloped in 2006 with one half dedicated to food and fortunately for the drinker contains a decent real ale bar.

The **Crown & Anchor, Mitre, Old Wellington** and **Sinclair's Oyster Bar** create a small enclave of pubs at one corner of **Exchange Square**. This area came into being after the destruction caused by the 1996 IRA bombing. Two of the pubs have been famously mobile over time. Sinclair's Oyster Bar and the Old Wellington once inhabited Shambles Square and had to be raised in the 1970s due to redevelopment. After the bombing that area was demolished due to the extensive damage caused and the two pubs were transported brick by brick to their current location. Along one side of Exchange Square is Triangle (the former Corn Exchange) now the home of many up-market brands. The Wheel of Manchester dominates the square and gives some good views around the city if you care to take a ride (greatcityattractions.com)

The area bounded by the **Hare & Hounds, Bluu, Common,** the **Wheatsheaf** and the **Smithfield Hotel & Bar** is the site of the various buildings that made up the former **Smithfield Market**, one of the largest in the country in its time. The rear entry to the Hare & Hounds is on the aptly named Salmon Street which leads to the cast iron gates of the Wholesale Fish Market of 1873. This is now a quiet courtyard containing the iron columns which used to support the

roof. Opposite **TV21** and next door to **Bluu** is the **Chinese Arts Centre** (chinese-arts-centre.org) based in Manchester, the city with the second largest Chinese community in the UK. The centre displays contemporary Chinese art and is part of the region's rich Chinese heritage. **Bluu** on the corner of Thomas Street and High Street is itself in the Market Buildings of 1878. These are former commercial chambers backing onto the Wholesale Fish Market. The stonework on the High Street side of the fish market contains a series of carved bas-reliefs depicting the lives of fishermen. Across from the **Wheatsheaf** is the **Craft and Design Centre** housed in the former Retail Fish Market. **The Smithfield Hotel & Bar** is on the opposite corner of Coop Street to the Smithfield Market Hall of 1857 which housed the butchers. The majority of the market has now disappeared but the remaining buildings are worthy of study with many fine architectural details.

The car park across from the **Unicorn** is the site of a warehouse of which one corner remains and is now an unusual musical sculpture. Next to the car park is **Afflecks Palace** an alternative shopping centre in a late 19th century shop and warehouse building. This contains an eclectic mix of stalls and shops in a kind of indoor bazaar spread over several floors. The **Ducie Bridge** sits in the shadow of the 'CIS' (Co-operative Insurance Society) building, Manchester's tallest until the arrival of the Beetham Tower. The majority of the area between the **Ducie Bridge**, Victoria station and Shudehill Interchange contains buildings belonging to the various arms of the 'Co-op' such as Wholesale and Banking. There are some fine early 20th century buildings here such as the 'Federation Building', 'Dantzic Building' and the rather dull sounding 'Block E'. 'Holyoake House' on Hanover Street houses the 'Co-op' archive which can be visited by appointment (co-op.ac.uk/our-heritage). These stand alongside some more modern buildings such as New Century House which housed the National Winter Ales Festival for a few years and the aforementioned CIS building. The new headquarters of the 'Co-op' is currently (late 2011) under construction in a large area behind the **Ducie Bridge** along Miller Street. When this opens all the old Co-op buildings will be renovated and converted for residential, commercial and leisure use.

Inn Sight of Manchester's History

The **Dutton Hotel** is hidden away behind the **Manchester Arena** which itself is built on top of **Victoria railway station**. This was opened in January 1844 by the Manchester and Leeds Railway Company and in May of that year was linked to the Liverpool and Manchester Railway. The current façade was completed in 1909 as the headquarters of the Lancashire and Yorkshire Railway. The Metrolink came to Victoria in 1992 when the former rail line to Bury was converted to tram use. The Manchester arena development, planned as part of Manchester's bid to host the 1996 Olympics, resulted in a large reduction in the size of the railway station was completed in 1995. It holds up to 21,000 people and hosts a wide range of events from concerts to wrestling and anything in between.

Just down the road from the **Gas Lamp** and directly across the River Irwell opposite the **Mark Addy** is the **People's History Museum** (phm.org.uk). It charts the history of democracy in Britain and the people's fight to get the vote, an important part of Manchester's history particularly after the industrial revolution. It combines the 1909 built pump house of the Manchester Hydraulic Power Company with a multimillion pound redevelopment that took place between 2007 and 2010.

The **Crescent** used to be known as the Red Dragon and is reputed to have been frequented by **Karl Marx** and **Frederick Engels** while developing their text on Marxist Theory. A lot of their theory came from observation of the industrial squalor of Salford and Manchester brought about by the industrial revolution. Appropriately along the Crescent from here is the **Working Class Movement Library** (wcml.org.uk) which records over 200 years of organising and campaigning by ordinary men and women.

Further information on the above and for the main Tourist Information Centre please contact:
Manchester Visitor Information Centre
45 - 50 Piccadilly Plaza, Portland Street, Manchester, M1 4BT
Opening times are Monday to Saturday, 9.30 am until 5.30 pm and Sunday, 10.30 am until 4.30 pm.
Telephone 0871 222 8223
Email: touristinformation@visitmanchester.com
Website: visitmanchester.com

OLD TOM

Seriously Strong

Alc 8.5% Vol

TASTING NOTES

Old Tom has a ripe vine fruit aroma with a delicious hint of chocolate as well as peppery hop resins. Port wine, dark malt chocolate and bitter hops fill the mouth while the long and complex finish offers an increasingly rich vinous fruitiness and a solid underpinning of bitter hops.

HISTORY

Old Tom is almost as old as the brewery itself. Over the years it has won some of the industry's most prestigious awards (30 in the last 25 years alone!) and is now recognised as one of the most famous strong ales both nationally and internationally where it is our fastest growing export beer.

f Find us on: **facebook.**

Robinsons Brewery

With an impressive lineage stretching from 1838 when William Robinson purchased the Unicorn Inn in Stockport, Robinsons Brewery has a strong heritage both in brewing and pub tenancy.

The passion and dedication of William Robinson and his descendants has seen Robinsons evolve into one of the UK's largest family brewers, with 380 pubs across Cumbria, Cheshire, Greater Manchester, Lancashire, Derbyshire and North Wales.

Our cask ales are all handcrafted at our Unicorn Brewery. We are most famous for our Old Tom ale, which is brewed from the original 1899 recipe and named after the brewery cat: we still use the original sketch of old tom as he basked in the sunshine in the brewery yard. We have a core range of ales including Unicorn and Dizzy Blonde and create limited edition seasonal ales, as well as supply supermarkets nationally with our bottled beers. Find Old Tom and Frederic Robinson on Facebook.

Massive investment into the brewery is underway with a new brew house and visitor centre in construction. This will give us the scope and flexibility to brew lots of really interesting craft beers. We will also be the proud owners of the largest Hop Nic in the World! (a device to extract all the flavours out of the hops and in to the beer).

The Brewery is due to be completed in February 2012, with tours commencing in the late summer of 2012 when the Visitor Centre will be open for business. As well as the visitor centre and brewery tours, the Brewery will also incorporate a training centre of excellence for our licensees (including training kitchen and cellar) and meeting / conference facilities available for corporate and private hire.

How to Use This Guide

This guide has been divided into several areas around the city, each with its own separate map for ease of reference. All the establishments which serve real ale are given full entries. The non-real ale ones which do not do so as yet appear in a separately after each main section.

Pub name ▶

Address ▶

Telephone number ▶

Website ▶

Opening hours ▶

Beers, ciders and perries ▶

Description ▶

Crown & Cushion

192 Corporation Street, M4 4DU

☎ (0161) 839 1844

⊕ josephholt.com

12-11 Mon-Sun

Joseph Holt Bitter, Mild

Originally a four roomed pub, it was opened up and the bar pushed to the back left hand corner when Joseph Holt took over from Whitbread. This was one of the oldest pubs in Manchester, having been built on the site of the Old Crown alehouse, which dates back to 1741.

Facilities and public transport ▶

❦✿❦⛽(M1,M2)

Explanation of Symbols Used Throughout This Guide

★ Pub with unspoilt interior

☆ Pub with some internal features

♨ Real fire

Q Quiet pub

❦ Family room

❀ Outdoor drinking / smoking area

⛺ Accommodation

(Lunchtime meals

▶ Evening meals

♿ Wheelchair access

🚌 Bus routes

♣ Traditional pub games played

♠ Real draught cider

Information boxes are scattered through this guide to provide you with further "Inn Sight" into some of Manchester's less obvious landmarks, or CAMRA

The information box will also point you toward of a pub in the vicinity of that point of interest.

The (M1, M2, M3) Metroshuttle free services are listed next to the bus routes 🚌 within the guide.

For more information about public transport in the Manchester area, please visit Transport for Greater Manchester (tfgm.com)

Overview Map

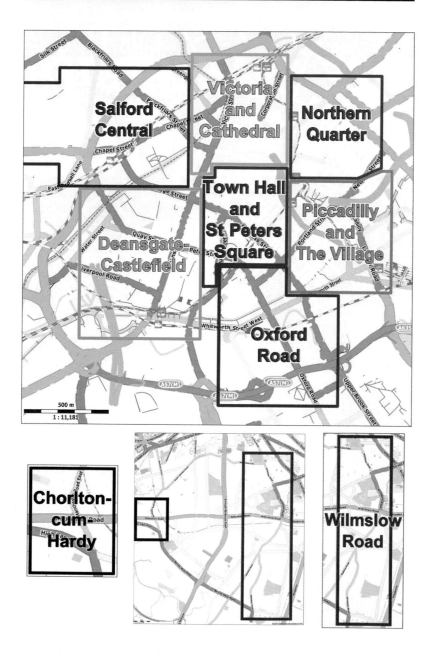

Salford Central

Victoria and Cathedral

Northern Quarter

Town Hall and St Peters Square

Deansgate-Castlefield

Piccadilly and The Village

Oxford Road

500 m

1 : 11,181

Chorlton-cum-Hardy

Wilmslow Road

LOVE MANCHESTER?
LOVE HOLTS

CELEBRATING REAL ALE SINCE 1849

WWW.JOSEPH-HOLT.COM

Town Hall and St Peter's Square

Manchester Town Hall

At the centre of Manchester is the magnificent neo-gothic Town Hall building located between Albert Square, home of Manchester's regular European markets (and other public festivals) and St Peter's Square where a Metrolink stop is located. To the west, the former Central Station is now Manchester Central exhibition, concert and conference venue. Manchester's China Town lies to the south east while the area to the north includes the exclusive King Street shopping area and the heart of Manchester's business district.

Attractions in This Area Include

Manchester Town Hall
Albert Square
Royal Exchange Theatre
Manchester Cenotaph
Manchester Art Gallery
Manchester Central and Conference Centre

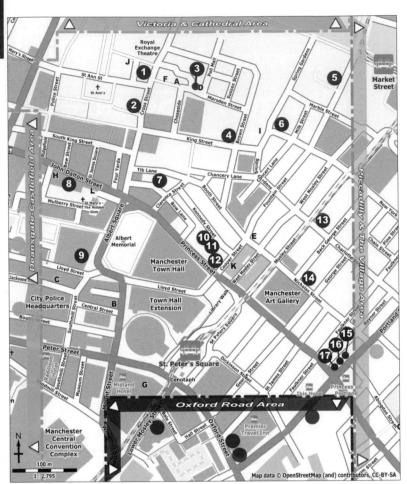

1	Corbières Wine Cavern	10	Vine Inn
2	Mr Thomas's Chop House	11	City Arms
3	Sam's Chop House	12	Waterhouse
4	All Bar One	13	Bank
5	Shakespeare	14	Seven Oaks
6	Brown's Bar & Brasserie	15	Grey Horse
7	Town Hall Tavern	16	Circus Tavern
8	Ape & Apple	17	Old Monkey
9	Slug & Lettuce		

All Bar One

73 King Street, M2 4NG
☎ 0161 830 2300 (Map: 4)
🌐 all-bar-one.co.uk
10-11 (12 Fri-Sat); 11-8 Sun
Sharps Doom Bar, Thwaites Original

One of a national chain of bars, this one has been established in Manchester since 1999. One large room with the bar covering half of one wall. It has the clean cut, open feel of many modern city bars with wooden furniture and light coloured walls.
🐾🐈🌙♿🚍(M1)

Ape & Apple

28-30 John Dalton Street, M2 6HQ
☎ 0161 839 9624 (Map: 8)
🌐 joseph-holt.com
12-11 (12 Fri-Sat); 12-9 Sun
Joseph Holt Bitter, Mild

Converted from a former bank in the late '90s this is a rare Joseph Holt outlet in the city centre and as such offers some of the cheapest drinks available. Well located between Deansgate and Albert Square, the pub attracts a wide clientele from shoppers to local office workers but retains a core of friendly regulars. Upstairs is a large dining room serving good value traditional pub fare at lunchtimes with a heated roof terrace attached with plentiful seating. Manchester's longest running free comedy club, Comedy Balloon, is held in the upstairs room every Wednesday evening with free admission. There is also a quiz night on Tuesdays.
🐈🌙♿🚍(M3)

Bank

57 Mosley Street, M2 3FF
☎ 0161 228 7560 (Map: 13)
🌐 nicholsonspubs.co.uk
10-11 (12 Fri-Sat); 10-11 Sun
Jennings Cumberland,

Thwaites Bomber + guests

The Bank occupies a handsome Greek revival building that is some 200 years old. Originally built to house the Portico Library (which still occupies the upper floor), the pub is in the former newsroom. Formerly the Forgery & Firkin, the Bank is part of the Nicholsons chain and so has something of an emphasis on cask beers with the regular offerings being supplemented by guests from around the country and often from unusual micros. The largely open-plan interior is nicely split up and retains many original features. In some respects it is redolent of a gentlemen's club, with a quiet, solid and purposeful air. Food is served 10 am until 10 pm Monday to Friday and 11 am until 10 pm on Saturday and

Sunday). The pub may close early if it is very quiet in the last hour.

Q◐⬤🚪(M1,M3)

Brown's Bar & Brasserie

1 York Street, M2 2AW
☎ 0161 819 1055 (Map: 6)
🌐 browns-restaurants.co.uk
8-11 (12 Fri); 10-12 Sat 10-10:30; Sun

Sharps Doom Bar, Thwaites Original

Until recently it was known as the Athenaeum, and then the Browns chain took over the premises earlier in 2011. Originally occupied by Parrs Bank, the building was designed by Charles Heathcote in 1902 and is a superb example of Edwardian baroque with some increasingly fashionable art nouveau detailing. A large room hosts the bar and relaxed seating areas. Since the takeover, the back rooms have been restored, in use as now hosting stunning dining rooms with one available for private hire. Although the real ale choice may be a little limited, the architecture is well worth seeing.

🦽◐♿🚪(M1)

Circus Tavern

86 Portland Street, M1 4GX
(Map:16)
12-12 (1 Fri-Sat); 12-11:30 Sun

Tetley Bitter

A tiny, two-roomed house, one which echoes times gone past in its layout. A small quadrant bar serves only one cask beer, whilst friendly waiting staff

guide you to a seat (space is at such a premium, that the table service really is a godsend here) in either the front room or back room (with television). Both rooms are plastered with hundreds of photos of footballers, boxers, comics and celebrities who have frequented the pub over the years. The back room's particular focus is on football material. Always popular with tourists, the Circus is a magnet for visitors to the town.

★🚪(M1,M3)

City Arms

46-48 Kennedy Street, M2 4BQ
☎ 0161 236 4610 (Map: 11)
11:30-11 (2 Fri); 12-12 Sat; 12-8 Sun

Tetley Bitter + guests

A traditional, compact two room pub with seven widely sourced guest beers along with the regular Tetley Bitter on offer. A real cider and at least seven malt whiskies always available, make this a very popular venue and a regular entry in CAMRA's Good Beer Guide for many years. There are pies available and always a friendly welcome. A recent addition is a smokers yard-cum-garden out at the back. Particularly busy on Fridays and Saturdays with a lot of regular clients, like a local in the city centre should be.

❀◐◑♣🚌(M3)

Corbières Wine Cavern

2 Half Moon Street, M2 7PB
☎ 0161 834 3381 (Map: 1)
12-11 (12 Thu-Sat) 12-10:30 Sun
Star Brewery Half Moon Bitter + guest

A hidden gem located along a side street, this cellar bar has a warm and cosy feel. It is accessed via a winding staircase which leads down into a 'mock-cavern' styled room. The unique subterranean surroundings and fantastic juke box gives the place a great atmosphere. Serving the local office trade for lunch, in the evenings it attracts a younger clientele in what can be a very lively and loud setting. Guest beers are most commonly from Boggart, Greenfield and Tetley and can be complemented with great lunchtime meals.

◐♣🚌(M1,M3)WiFi

Grey Horse

80 Portland Street, M1 4QX
☎ 0161 236 1874 (Map: 15)
🌐 hydesbrewery.co.uk
11-11 (11:30 Fri-Sat); 12-10:30 Sun
Hydes Original, Mild + seasonals

A friendly single roomed old pub, probably converted from early 19th century weavers' cottages, and named after an act in the circus that used to overwinter in this block. It has a light, clean interior with red upholstered bench seating and stools, and dark laminate floor. Entered via steps from the street, it may prove difficult for disabled persons. A tiny, heated outdoor yard at the rear can seat two people. Certainly one of the smallest pubs in the city, it can get busy on football match days, when space is at a premium.

🚌(M1,M3)

Mr Thomas's Chop House

52 Cross Street, M2 7AR
☎ 0161 832 2245   (Map: 2)
⊕ thevictorianchophousecompany.com
11-11 Mon-Sat; 12-9 Sun
Joseph Holt, JW Lees and Robinsons range + guests

One of only a handful of Manchester pubs listed in CAMRA's National Inventory. A long, narrow room divided by green tiled arches leads from the entrance along the bar and opens up into two further rooms, these further divided by the same arches at the back. In the rear room there is a magnificent ceramic fireplace. The pub is famed for its food and is popular with theatre goers to the nearby Royal Exchange.
★⅍✿◗🚆(M1)

Over the last few years Manchester has developed its Christmas market into one of the largest in the country. Spread out from Exchange Square into St. Ann's Square and from Albert Square into Lincoln Square it now covers a large area with stalls from all over the UK and Europe. German beer tents are a feature for the drinker.

Mr Thomas's Chop House, another fine historic gem, miraculously escaped virtually unscathed from the IRA bomb of 1996.

Old Monkey

90-92 Portland Street, M1 4GX
☎ 0161 237 3291   (Map: 17)
⊕ joseph-holt.com
12-11 (11:45 Fri-Sat); 12-9 Sun
Joseph Holt Bitter, Mild + seasonal

Holts' first ever new-build house in the city and situated on the site of the Queens Arms beer house, it opened in 1993 to great acclaim. Set on two floors with the downstairs being the main engine of trade, a mostly standing up drinking area. Meanwhile upstairs (which opens from 12 pm until 6 pm on Mondays to Thursdays and all day on Fridays and Saturdays, closing on Sundays) has its own bar, and serves the food in a comfortable and intimate environment. The upstairs windows provide you with great views of the bustle of Princess Street junction. The success of the 'Monkey' inspired Holts' to open the Ape & Apple nearby. Food is on offer 12 pm until 6 pm daily.
◗🚆(M1,M3)

> Just off Cross Street lies Back Pool Fold which in 1586 was home to the town 'ducking stool'. This was "...for the punishment of Lewed women and Scoldes", so behave yourself!
>
> *Sam's Chop House is one of two 'Victorian chop houses' within the city.*

Sam's Chop House

Chapel Walks, off Cross Street, M2 1HN
☎ 0161 834 3210 (Map: 3)
🌐 thevictorianchophousecompany.com
11-11 (12 Fri-Sat); 12-9 Sun
Coach House Sam's Best Bitter, Flowers IPA

Stairs lead down from the entrance to a room with a low ceiling and a restaurant attached. Sam's dates back to 1872 and has been on the current premises since the 1950s. Steeped in history and once patronised by L S Lowry, who is commemorated with a life-sized statue at the bar. On Wednesday nights a human jukebox and guitarist plays requests.
⌦🐕♿🍴(M1)

Seven Oaks

5 Nicholas Street, M1 4HL
☎ 0161 237 1233 (Map: 14)
12-12 (9 Fri-Sat); 12-12 Sun
Black Sheep Best Bitter, Timothy Taylor Landlord

A distinctive white glazed

faience block exterior with an architectural ironwork tree and a small ironwork balcony, close to the Chinatown area. You enter via the steps from the street into a single, well furnished room surrounding a traditional bar in dark wood with cut glass mirrors. The dark wood theme is echoed in panelling at the stairs leading up to a far larger function room that is used when the pub is more crowded. All in all this is a very traditional, friendly and pleasant pub. Although it opens quite late, club members can drink till 7 am. Toilets are in the basement, so not really suitable for disabled customers. Food served is available on weekdays between 12 pm and 3 pm.
🍴🍽(M1,M3)

Shakespeare

16 Fountain Street, M2 2AA

☎ 0161 834 5515   (Map: 5)

🌐 clovertaverns.co.uk

11:30-11 Mon-Sat; 11:30-11 Sun

Boddington Bitter, Wells &
Young Bombardier

A pub has occupied this site since 1721, although the frontage of the building was brought from Chester in the early 1900s. Inside, the room has been opened out somewhat, with a main bar facing the entrance and television screens and jukebox. It serves up to three cask ales and provides food at most times and is especially popular with the shopping crowds. There are ghostly tales too, the reputed haunting of a servant girl who set fire to herself whilst lighting the inn's candles and that of a chef who hanged himself after attacking her.

◖ WiFi

Slug & Lettuce

Heron House, Albert Square, M2 5HD

☎ 0161 839 3604   (Map: 9)

🌐 slugandlettuce.co.uk

11-11; 10-12 Fri-Sat 10-10:30 Sun

Thwaites Wainwright, Wells &
Young Bombardier

A long open-plan one room establishment incorporates a bar, a restaurant, plus a small lounge area. A long veranda dominates its exterior with outdoor tables and seating which overlooks the wide area in front of Alfred Waterhouse's impressive Town Hall façade. Note that cask ale may not always be available and there is no disabled access to the bar

serving area.

🍽✤◖⟡🚃(M3)

Town Hall Tavern

20 Tib Lane, M2 4JA

☎ 0161 832 3550   (Map: 7)

12-12 Mon-Sat; 12-12 Sun

Caledonian Deuchars IPA,
Timothy Taylor Landlord

After undergoing many name changes and reincarnations, it seems to have stabilised after another recent refurbishment. The rooms are set on several split levels with some original features having survived in its present form.

Q🍽⟡🚃(M3)

Vine Inn

42-44 Kennedy Street, M2 4BQ

☎ 0161 237 9740   (Map: 10)

🌐 vineinnmanchester.com

11-11 Mon-Sat (12 Fri); Closed Sun

Timothy Taylor Landlord,
Wychwood Hobgoblin

A traditional hostelry, portraying an impressive tiled, stained glass exterior. Rumoured to have begun life as Manchester's oldest brothel, it is evidently spacious, extending to over three levels inside. The walls upstairs are adorned with images of old Manchester while downstairs has a range of old enamelled and painted signs.

Darts, dominoes and board games are available on request from the bar. The downstairs room with a separate bar serves meals weekday lunchtimes and is available for hire evenings and weekends.

⟨🍺♿♣🚆(M3)

Waterhouse
71 Princess Street, M2 4EG
☎ 0161 200 5380   (Map: 12)
8-12 Mon-Sat; 8-12 Sun
Elland Waterhouse IPA,
Phoenix Wobbly Bob + guests

This Wetherspoons, unlike so many of the chain, is split into multiple rooms with some character. There are 10 hand pumps featuring local micro breweries with Phoenix Wobbly Bob and its own specially brewed Waterhouse IPA from Elland Brewery permanently available alongside Wetherspoons house ales (check behind the pillar to the left of the bar for these beers). Regular 'Meet The Brewer' evenings are held and good relations with a number of breweries often result in specials and rebranded ales being available. A range of Westons' Ciders are normally available.

Q🛏️🍴◑♿🍴🚆(M3)WiFi

Other Pubs and Bars in This Area
Bacchanalia
15-17 Chapel Walks, M2 1HN
☎ 0161 819 1997   (Map: A)
Beluga
Lawrence Buildings, 2 Mount Street, M2 5WQ
☎ 0161 833 3339   (Map: B)

Cellar Vie
29 Lloyd Street, M2 5WA
☎ 0161 834 9696   (Map: C)
Chaophraya Bar
19 Chapel Walks, M2 1HN
☎ 0161 832 8342   (Map: D)
Crown
89 Fountain Street, M2 2EF
☎ 0161 237 3506   (Map: E)
Grinch
Old Half Moon Chambers 5-7 Chapel Walks, M2 1HN
☎ 0161 907 3210   (Map: F)
Midland Hotel
16 Peter Street, M60 2DS
☎ 0161 236 3333   (Map: G)
Restaurant Bar and Grill
14 John Dalton Street, M2 6JR
☎ 0161 839 2005   (Map: H)
Room
81 King Street, M2 4AH
☎ 0161 839 2005   (Map: I)
Sandinista Cantina Bar
2 Old Bank Chambers, 2 Old Bank Street, M2 7PF
☎ 0161 832 9955   (Map: J)
Tiger Lounge
Waldorf House, 5 Cooper Street, M2 2FW
☎ 0161 236 6007   (Map: K)
Vertigo
36 John Dalton Street, M2 6LE
☎ 0161 839 9907   (Map: L)

Victoria and Cathedral

Manchester Cathedral

Victoria station is served by many trains from the north, east and west. Manchester's 20,000 seat Arena is adjacent to the station. South of the station is Manchester Cathedral and beyond that the New Cathedral Street and Exchange Square areas, built on the ruins of the 1996 IRA bomb and now home to Harvey Nichols, Selfridges and Marks & Spencer department stores. On the other side of Exchange Square are The Printworks entertainment centre, built on the site of the former Mirror printing works and the Arndale Centre, home to most major name stores.

Attractions in This Area Include

Victoria Station	The Triangle
Manchster Cathedral	The Printworks
Arndale Centre	Manchester Arena
New Cathedral Street	National Football
Exchange Square	Museum (opening *2012*)

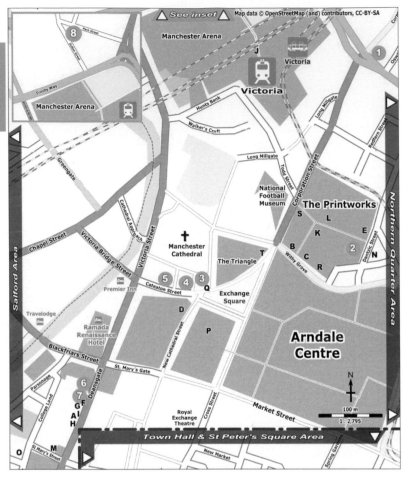

1 Ducie Bridge
2 Lloyds No 1
3 Old Wellington
4 Mitre
5 Crown & Anchor
6 Slug & Lettuce
7 Moon Under Water
8 Dutton Hotel

Heritage Pubs

Heritagepubs.org.uk

CAMRA is wholly committed to doing all it can to protect our dwindling stock of intact historic pub interiors. This website lists National and regional lists of pubs of historic interest

Crown & Anchor

4-8 Cateaton Street, M3 1SQ
☎ 0161 834 7046   (Map: 5)
⊕ joseph-holt.com
12-11:30 (12:30 Sat); 12-9 Sun
**Joseph Holt Bitter, Mild +
seasonal**

This was pretty much a working man's pub until a major refurbishment in 2003 turned it into a much smarter bar with a food operation. This was probably to bring it in line with the other pubs on the relatively recently created Exchange Square which is now a popular drinking location. It can get crowded on weekend evenings or before events at the nearby Manchester arena. It serves the full range of Holts' beers from a central bar and is a split level pub with an area of comfy sofas at the back along the top level. The lower level had maintained a public bar feel, but following further refurbishment a couple of years ago this is no longer the case. Good value lunchtime meals are available, but be wary of the fact that if you want to drink on the pavement seats outside, you will have to use a plastic glass as is mandatory throughout Manchester's city centre establishments. Despite the refurbishment it still retains its traditional exterior with its stone clad name at the top of the building.
⏤☗❀◖🖵 (M2)

Possibly the most famous post box in the country stands on Corporation Street across from the Arndale Centre. Due to its survival at the centre of the IRA bombing of June 1996 it appeared in the media worldwide and now carries a plaque commemorating its history.

The Crown & Anchor (one of two pubs bearing the same name in the city) is close by the Manchester Wheel in Exchange Square.

Ducie Bridge

152 Corporation Street, M4 4DU
☎ 0161 831 9725   (Map: 1)
⊕ theduciebridge.com
12-1 Mon-Sat; 12-1 Sun
**Joseph Holt Bitter, Howard
Town Wren's Nest + guest**

This building has a fine ornate red brick exterior with a corner entrance and main door, leading to a large open plan lounge with a small stage in the rear corner, flanked by a long bar. There is a snug to the right of the main door

and a large upstairs function room. In addition to the cask ale on offer, there are some interesting Continental beers including those of Anchor and Karmeliet, as bottle conditioned brews. Quiz nights are held on Thursdays, with live music on Fridays and Saturdays. It started selling real ale again in early 2011 after the closure of the nearby Crown & Cushion. The eponymous bridge across the road junction crosses the Manchester and Leeds Railway as well as the now hidden River Irk.
🍴◖♣ WiFi

Next to one of the main entrances to Victoria railway station is a fine tiled Lancashire and Yorkshire Railway map showing coast to coast services from Manchester. This sits above a First World War memorial featuring a tableau of George and the Dragon.

The Ducie Bridge lies in the shadow of the tall CIS building.

Dutton Hotel

37 Park Street, M3 1EU
☎ 0161 834 4508   (Map: 8)
🌐 hydesbrewery.co.uk
12-11 Mon-Sat; 12-10 Sun
Hydes Original

Overlooking the now demolished Boddingtons brewery this is one of the city's few remaining street corner locals. A wedge shaped structure built on the angle of two street junctions; it has been a pub since at least the 1880s. The interior was altered in 1979 from several rooms into the semi open plan format we see today, with three small areas served from the central bar and the front room also has a large anvil in

the corner window. The two back rooms have a television each and darts are played in the smaller of the two. Unusually a collection of blow lamps are festooned on a lot of the ceiling space. Ironically this Hydes' pub used to be popular with Boddingtons brewery workers as well as prison officers from the nearby Strangeways. During the prison riots of 1984 this became a drinking base for the media. It is now a very handy place for those visiting the Manchester Arena and Victoria railway station.
Q♣🚃 (M2)

Lloyds No 1

Printworks, 27 Withy Grove, M4 2BS
☎ 0161 817 2980   (Map: 2)
🌐 jdwetherspoon.co.uk
9-12 (1 Wed-Thu; 2 Fri-Sat); 9-12 Sun
Greene King Abbot Ale,
Ruddles + guests

Although the J D Wetherspoon website calls this pub the 'Seven Stars' there is no apparent indication of this inside or outside the pub. The main bar is along the right hand wall as you enter from the Printworks and there is an upstairs bar devoid of handpumps but the area provides extra seating. There are televisions with sub-titles and no sound, as piped music is played. The lighting inside is low apart from the bar area and this can be very busy, especially at weekends and evenings.
🍴◖♿♣🚃 (M2) WiFi

Mitre

1-3 Cathedral Gates, M3 1SW
☎ 0161 834 4128   (Map: 4)
11-11 Mon-Sat; 12-10:30 Sun
Timothy Taylor Landlord,
Jennings Cumberland

This is a large residential hotel with two bars, presently the bar fronting onto Exchange Square is the only one that is open and selling real ale. There are lots of comfy and maybe some would say unusual seating, styling itself as a 'boutique' pub. The hotel itself is a Grade II listed building, dating from 1815 with a mixture of sandstone and Jacobean styles. It was refurbished and reopened in December 2009 and sold to Enterprise Inns in late 2010.

☎☆🚪◐❤️🚻(M2)WiFi

Moon Under Water
68-74 Deansgate, M3 2FN
☎ 0161 236 0564   (Map: 7)
🌐 jdwetherspoon.co.uk
9-12 (1 Thu-Sat); 9-12 Sun
Greene King Abbot Ale,
Ruddles + guests

A huge cavernous Wetherspoons in what was a former picture house. Spread over two floors it is still possible to find a secluded corner amongst its three bars. The decor is in the Art Deco style with a splendid stained glass window on the back staircase depicting the moon under water. The various bars are served by separate cellars so there is often a very varied range of ales. As with all J D Wetherspoon houses, you generally know what you're going to get, but this one surprises on each visit and this appeals, to bring in customers of all ages.

Q☆◐❤️🚻🚪(M1,M2)

Old Wellington
4 Cathedral Gates, M3 1SW
☎ 0161 839 5179   (Map: 3)
🌐 nicholsonspubs.co.uk
10-11 (12 Fri-Sat); 10-10:30 Sun
Jennings Cumberland,
Thwaites Bomber

This is probably Manchester's oldest inn dating back to 1552, when it was close to the old market which was then the centre of the town at that time. Despite its age it has been fairly mobile in recent times and along with Sinclair's Oyster Bar it was raised on a concrete raft in a 1970s redevelopment of the old Shambles to make way for an underground access road. Both pubs moved again after the IRA bombing of 1996, this time about 120 yards to their current location

and reopened in 1999; sensitive and expensive renovation was carried out during both these moves. The pub has literally settled into its new location and sells up to eight real ales from its ground floor bar. There are two upper floors which are mainly given over to a popular restaurant operation although you are able to sit and drink upstairs if you wish.

Q ➲ ✿◑ ♿ 🚌 (M2)

Slug & Lettuce

64-66 Deansgate, M3 2EN
☎ 0161 839 0985   (Map: 6)
🌐 slugandlettuce.co.uk
10-11 (1 Fri-Sat); 10-11 Sun
Timothy Taylor Landlord,
Wells & Young Bombardier

A listed building which dates from the Georgian era and an interior dominated with a large single room. This features a classic high ceiling and columns which are sub-divided into a bar, restaurant and lounge area housing contemporary furnishings.

➲ ✿◑ ♿ 🚌 (M1,M2)

Other Pubs and Bars in This Area

Café Rouge (Deansgate)
84 Deansgate, M3 2ER
☎ 0161 839 0414   (Map: A)
Café Rouge (Printworks)
Printworks, 27 Withy Grove, M4 2BS
0161 832 7749   (Map: B)
Hard Rock Café
Printworks, 27 Withy Grove, M4 2BS
☎ 0161 831 6700   (Map: C)
Harvey Nichols Second Floor Bar
21 Cathedral Street, M1 1AD
☎ 0161 828 8898   (Map: D)
Henry J Beans
Printworks, 27 Withy Grove, M4 2BS
☎ 0161 827 7820   (Map: E)

La Tasca
76 Deansgate, M3 2FW
☎ 0161 834 8234   (Map: F)
Label
78 Deansgate, M3 2FW
☎ 0161 833 1878   (Map: G)
Las Iguanas
84 Deansgate, M3 2ER
☎ 0161 819 2606   (Map: H)
Living Room
80 Deansgate, M3 2ER
☎ 0161 832 0083   (Map: I)
Metro Bar
Victoria Station Concourse, M3 1NY
(Map: J)
Norwegian Blue
Printworks, 27 Withy Grove, M4 2BS
☎ 0161 839 1451   (Map: K)
Old Orleans
Printworks, 27 Withy Grove, M4 2BS
☎ 0161 839 4430   (Map: L)
Prohibition
2-10 St Mary's Street, M3 2LB
☎ 0161 831 9326   (Map: M)
Pulse Sports Bar
Victoria Buildings, Dantzic Street, M4 2AD
☎ 0161 833 0330   (Map: N)
Revolution
Arkwright House Parsonage Gardens, M3 2LF
☎ 0161 839 9675   (Map: O)
Selfridges Moet Bar 2nd Floor, 1 Exchange Sq, M3 1BD
(Map: P)
Sinclairs Oyster Bar
2 Cathedral Gates, M3 1SW
☎ 0161 834 0430   Map: Q)
Tiger Tiger
Printworks, 27 Withy Grove, M4 2BS
☎ 0161 385 8080   (Map: R)
Waxy O'Connors
Printworks, 27 Withy Grove, M4 2BS
☎ 0161 835 1210   (Map: S)
Zinc
The Triangle, 37 Hanging Ditch, M4 3TR
☎ 0161 827 4200   (Map: T)

Are You a CAMRA Member?

You walk into a pub and glance up and down the bar for the presence of the distinctive handpumps. Your heart lifts as you see a recognisable pump clip, or falls to the floor when you notice the bare handle. Sound familiar?

You order your beer, wait and let it settle. You delight in the clarity of the beer, and the creamy head that adorns the top of every great pint, pulled in the right way. You savour the first sip, because it's the first sip that counts. Maybe you take a second to get a nose full of that distinctive hoppy aroma. Not a drop is wasted.

Maybe you get chatting to someone at the bar. Favourite beers, local breweries and recent beer festivals are always the topic of conversation. Strangers bound together by a common interest. It is magical to walk into an unfamiliar pub and find a 'friend' at the bar.

Consider this – real ale, when consumed in moderation, is a most enjoyable drink. Real ale is thriving because people look for quality and integrity in the product and the organisations that supply them. Modern corporations, who without hesitation put profit before customers and money saving before quality, should take note. CAMRA is growing everyday, and so is the influence of its 129,000 plus supporters.

What about the beer brewed on your doorstep? We call it LocAle. Greater Manchester produces some of the best beers in the country. We should be proud of this fact and order a pint whenever we see it

The former Great Northern Railway Warehouse was a vast construction running along the southern end of Deansgate on one side and Manchester Central on the other. It was built from 1896 and 1899 to provide an interchange between the canals and the expanding railway and road systems of a rapidly growing city. You may be surprised to learn when viewing it from Deansgate that much of it has been demolished. It now houses various shops and leisure facilities including a multi-screen cinema.

The Deansgate is next to Manchester's tallest structure, the Beetham Tower.

Are You a CAMRA Member?

served, so everyone benefits. Reducing 'beer miles' ensures you can invest in your local economy. This can only breed an increased sense of local identity and pride.

CAMRA, the campaign for real ale was founded in 1971 by a group of four drinkers who were apposed to the growing mass production of beer. CAMRA promote small brewing and pub businesses, help to reform licensing laws and campaign to reducing tax on beer. It also makes an effort to promote less common varieties of beer and other traditionally brewed drinks including **stout, porter, mild,** traditional **cider** and **perry.**

So, are you a CAMRA member? The answer does not really matter.

To be honest, if you have taken the time to read this article, then you are already a CAMRA member – you may have just forgotten to join!

Your membership form is on page **44.**

With thanks to George Symes and Out Inn Cheshire for the kind use of this article.

Northern Quarter

Afflecks Palace

The Northern Quarter used to be one of the main market and warehouse areas of the city and was neglected for a long time as their influence waned. However this saw cheaper rents available that attracted the more artistic and bohemian characters and led to the area becoming the more creative part of the city with the Afflecks Palace retail emporium at its centre. Coupled with recent regeneration including conversion of many of the old premises into flats the area is now bustling and vibrant. This has seen a mini explosion in the number of bars; many of these provide a fine array of real ales. Where the Northern Quarter meets Manchester Arndale Centre is the Arndale Market Hall.

Attractions in This Area Include

Shudehill Interchange
Picadilly Gardens Bus Station
Manchester Police Museum
Chinese Arts Centre
Manchester Design and Craft Centre
Afflecks Palace
Band on the Wall

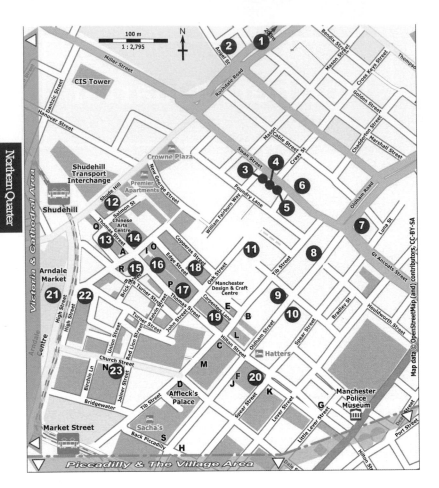

1 Marble Arch Inn	13 TV21
2 Angel	14 Bluu
3 Smithfield Hotel & Bar	15 Odd
4 Burton Arms Hotel	16 Bay Horse
5 Band on the wall	17 57 Thomas Street
6 Bar Fringe	18 Common
7 Crown & Kettle	19 Millstone
8 City	20 Soup Kitchen
9 Gullivers	21 MicroBar
10 Castle Hotel	22 English Lounge
11 Wheatsheaf	23 Unicorn
12 Hare & Hounds	

57 Thomas Street

57 Thomas Street, M4 1NA
☎ 0161 832 0521   (Map: 17)
🌐 marblebeers.co.uk
11-12 Mon-Sat; 11-12 Sun
Marble Beers + seasonals

Opened in 2010 this was converted from a shop into a small one room bar. It is owned by the Marble brewery and sells the full range of Marble beers, although not all of them may be available at any one time. Up to four beers are served straight from the casks that are situated on the bar top, as there is no cellar. The bar takes up most of the right hand wall and there is a long table with seating in front of this, making it a little cramped. There is a small more relaxed seating area to the left as you enter as well as some pavement tables and chairs - subject to the renowned Manchester weather. Bottled Belgian and German beers, an interesting variety of meals, snacks and cakes are on sale at all times.
🏵◗&

Angel

6 Angel Street, M4 4BR
☎ 0161 833 4786   (Map: 2)
🌐 theangelmanchester.com
11-12 Mon-Sat; Closed Sun
Bob's White Lion + guests

Formerly the much revered Beer House but now forging its own identity, acknowledged by an award of the 2010 CAMRA branch Pub Of The Year. After having been closed for some time and in the doldrums, this is once more a thriving free house. It serves the recently developed apartments just north of the city centre as well as those with a penchant for quality real ale. Ground floor drinkers are catered for in an L-shaped room with bare floorboards and a warming fire in winter. The bar is adorned with ten handpumps and a beer range that is ever changing and sourced from all over the country with small breweries championed; two of these are reserved for real cider and perry. Upstairs there is a well established restaurant and there is a quiz night on Mondays.
🏚🏵◗🍎👥

Band On The Wall

25 Swan Street, M4 5JZ
☎ 0161 834 1786   (Map: 5)
🌐 bandonthewall.org
5:30-Late Mon-Fri; (Sat - see gig guide) Closed Sun
Hydes Original, seasonal + guests

Also incorporating the Picturehouse bar, this is one of Manchester's most famous live music venues. It closed and underwent a complete and not inexpensive refurbishment, reopening in September 2009 to a great fanfare and once again reverberates to the sound of many live bands. Upon its revival, there appeared a public bar adjacent to the main venue, this being the aforementioned Picturehouse. Located in a Grade II listed building this is open to casual visitors as well as providing an overspill for the main venue. Real ales are sold in both areas, although you will need a gig ticket to access the bar in the venue. Check the website or the music press for further information.
🍴🍺♿WiFi

Bar Fringe

8 Swan Street, M4 5JN
☎ 0161 835 3815   (Map: 6)
12-12 (12:30 Fri-Sat); 12-12 Sun
Up to 5 guest ales

This is a popular and eclectic Belgian style bar, a long narrow one roomed affair with a small raised seating area as you enter. There are five hand pumps dispensing beers from local breweries and much farther afield. A good range of draught and bottled continental beers are also available, as well as real cider. The eccentric décor will occupy you as you imbibe with its collection of ornamental rats and customised Tin Tin cartoons amongst other paraphernalia. Above the entrance there is even a motorcycle in a 'how did that get there?' position. The beer garden at the rear is a surprisingly pleasant place to relax with a pint ... and listen out for the Cuckoo clock too!
🏺🍺🍎

Bay Horse

35-37 Thomas Street, M4 1NA
☎ 0161 661 1041   (Map: 16)
⊕ thebayhorsepub.co.uk
12-11 (1 Fri-Sat); 12-1 Sun
Guest ale

A long time ago this was a Wilsons pub - remember them? In those less than halcyon days it was more noted for its strippers than for its beer and thankfully today has re-emerged as one of the new breed of stylish Northern Quarter bars. Entry is gained up some steps leading into the main room with the bar in the right hand corner. The furniture is a mixture of tables with wooden chairs, comfy chairs and a chaise-longue, providing a relaxed atmosphere. A flight of stairs in the left hand corner leads down into a room featuring a pool table with a separate bar, although there isn't a handpump for cask ale down here.
❀◐♣

Bluu

85 High Street, M4 1FS
☎ 0161 839 7195   (Map: 14)
⊕ bluu.co.uk
12-12 (1 Thu; 2 Fri-Sat); 12-12 Sun
Marston's EPA + seasonals

A modern split-level café bar in what has become one of the trendiest areas of the city. It predominantly attracts a young clientele in the evenings where there are several drinking areas which include sofas and more intimate booths, from where you can admire the eclectic décor including their unusual glass encased columns. Large windows give views onto the Thomas Street and High Street thoroughfares on one side and the square on the other. Informative menus include details of regular food and drink offers. After a gap of a few years it now has five handpumps serving up to three real ales from the Marston's stable. An excellent list of non-alcoholic cocktails (mocktails!) complements the expertly mixed selection of traditional ones. It was bought by the Marston's pub company in 2006 although it does not give the appearance of being a chain pub.
❀◐&WiFi

Burton Arms Hotel

31 Swan Street, M4 5JZ
☎ 0161 834 3455   (Map: 4)
⊕ burtonarmshotel.co.uk
12-11 (1 Fri-Sat); 12-12 Sun
Joseph Holt Bitter, Thwaites Bitter

This is a small and friendly local pub despite its darkish interior, with entertainment most evenings where free and easy or karaoke features. There is a long narrow room with the bar halfway along the right hand wall and a small raised area to

the right on entry has seating, unless used for television viewing or the entertainment. There are several televisions for showing sport amongst other things and a small room at the rear has a pool table. Accommodation at reasonable rates is available.

❀☙◔♣ WiFi

Castle Hotel

66 Oldham Street, M4 1LE
☎ 0161 237 9485   (Map: 10)
🌐 thecastlehotel.info
1-12 Mon-Sat; 12-8 Sun
Robinsons Old Tom, Mild +
seasonals

This is the city centre's only Robinsons' tied house and has been part of their estate since 1946. The Grade II listed building underwent an extensive and sensitive refurbishment that was finally completed in October 2010. This pub is well worth a visit to view many of its fine features, such as its brown tiled frontage then on entering via the right hand lobby you cross the mosaic castle in the floor. This leads into the small vault and facing is the fine mahogany topped bar with an equally splendid tiled front. Along the corridor there is a pleasant snug replete with piano and a larger back room that hosts live bands and other artistic events. In this latter room, the skylight has been restored, formerly hidden by a false ceiling for many years. Fortunately for the drinker the beer quality is maintained as well as the building with the majority of the Robinsons' range dispensed, as well as Westons cider, on its seven handpumps.

❀◔

City

133 Oldham Street, M4 1LN
(Map: 8)
11-11 Mon-Sat 11-11 Sun
Acorn City Pride + guest

A Grade II listed building, which was refurbished after a fire in 2007. It consists of a single long lounge with a bar along the right hand wall and can be accessed by the main entrance on Oldham Street or the back door on Tib Street. The interesting frontage is dominated by the Royal coat of arms and a tableau celebrating the arrival of William III and Mary II and being welcomed by Britannia. The pub rejoined the real ale fold in 2009 after a long absence and usually has three ales on tap, one being the house ale from Acorn brewery, plus varying guests. It tends to be busier during the day and the pub is sport orientated, also holding a popular karaoke on Saturdays.

♣

Common

39-41 Edge Street, M4 1HW
☎ 0161 832 9245 (Map: 18)
🌐 aplacecalledcommon.co.uk
11-12 (2 Thu-Sat); 11-12 Sun
Up to two guest ales

This bar opened in converted shop premises in 2005 and expanded into next door five years later. The new room is known as the 'Kestrel Suite' and whilst normally open to anyone, it can be hired out for private functions. Real ale did not feature until 2010 and now there are two regular guest beers from a variety of brewers both near and far. There is also a selection of interesting bottled beers, mainly from the USA. Good quality food is served until 10 pm all week. The building itself is not of great architectural merit - so in order to make it interesting - turn the whole place into an ever changing art gallery! Pretty much all the wall space is used up and as such it is always worth a look around; in fact if you think you have something to contribute then check out the website regarding submissions. They generally attract a younger clientele, but the staff is always friendly whoever you are. Sign up as a member and get discounts on food and drink which includes their real ales.
◐▶

Crown & Kettle

2 Oldham Road, M4 5FE
☎ 0161 236 29 (Map: 7)
🌐 crownandkettle.com
11-11 (12 Fri-Sat); 12-11 Sun
Up to four guest ales

This Grade II listed free house was reopened in 2005 after 16 years of closure, by some enterprising developers. This was done in cooperation with English Heritage with particular attention to the fine and unusual ceiling. It quickly gained a reputation for selling up to four quality beers from far and wide. The central bar serves a large drinking hall, a small vault and a smart modern snug at the rear. Live music makes an occasional appearance and food is served up to 4 pm. The pub itself dates from around 1800 and was seen as quite a prosperous commodity in the mid 19th century. This was due to its being located at its road junctions, a close proximity to the nearby to the once thriving Smithfield markets area. Prior to closure in 1989 it had been famous for its life-size statue of Winston Churchill and use of wood panelling from the R101 airship; one can only wonder what became of Winston.
♣◑♿♥

English Lounge

64-66 High Street, M4 1EA
☎ 0161 832 4824 (Map: 22)
12-11 (1 Fri-Sat); 12-10:30 Sun
Black Sheep Best Bitter,
Marston's Pedigree + guests

Opposite the Arndale Centre Market and over the years this pub has seen many name changes and refurbishments, now having settling on its present one for the last several years. A large L-shaped open plan room and bar with wooden flooring and pillars divide up the areas and there is a mixture

of different coloured furniture, tables and chairs. Subdued lighting and piped music is featured, whilst upstairs there is a function room, the 'library' for providing additional seating and an outside smoking terrace. Real ales are dispensed from six handpumps but not all may be available all of the time. Lunchtime and evening meals are also a feature.
✿◖◗

Gullivers

109 Oldham Street, M4 1LW
(Map: 9)
5-1 (3 Fri-Sat); 5-1 Sun
JW Lees seasonal

This reopened in late 2010 essentially as an alternative music venue. Upon entry from the street there is a long narrow front room with the bar half way along the wall on the right. Immediately to the left is a small raised area for DJ's or karaoke. Along the left side is seating with a variety of gig posters on the wall above and just beyond the bar on the left is a small room with more relaxed seating, with the upstairs of the pub being converted into the live music area. Previously, this pub was known as the Albert and then the Grenadier, when owned by Wilsons brewery.

Hare & Hounds

46 Shudehill, M4 4AA
☎ 0161 832 4737   (Map:12)
11-11:30 Mon-Sat; 12-10:30 Sun
Joseph Holt Bitter

A Grade II listed traditional pub dating from around 1800 that attracts a mostly mature clientele. The pub was remodelled in 1925 and the frontage has a blue-brown glazed tiled covering. The interior also has tiling and the woodwork is as it was then, becoming such a rare survivor. It sits opposite Shudehill Interchange betwixt the contrasting drinking areas of the Northern Quarter and the Printworks. At the front there is a basic vault and a well used drinking corridor leads to a plusher back lounge. It features regular karaoke on Sundays and other musical events. There is an upstairs function room.
★🖼(M2)

Marble Arch Inn

73 Rochdale Road, M4 4HY
☎ 0161 832 5914   (Map: 1)
⊕ marblebeers.co.uk
12-11:30 (12:30 Sat); 12-12 Sun
Marble Pint, Manchester Bitter + guests

On approaching this real ale pub, stop and take a moment to observe the impressively stacked roof. Then enjoy the grandeur of the eponymous front entrance, although the

MARBLE
BEERS LTD

Your CAMRA Membership Form

For more information about CAMRA, please see the article "Are You a CAMRA Member?" on pages 33 and 34.

A Campaign of Two Halves

Fair deal on beer tax

Save Britain's Pubs!

Join CAMRA Today

Complete the Direct Debit form and you will receive 15 months membership for the price of 12 and a fantastic discount on your membership subscription.

Alternatively you can send a cheque payable to CAMRA Ltd with your completed form, visit www.camra.org.uk/joinus or call 01727 867201. All forms should be addressed to Membership Department, CAMRA, 230 Hatfield Road, St Albans, AL1 4LW.

Your Details

Title _____ Surname _____

Forename(s) _____

Date of Birth (dd/mm/yyyy) _____

Address _____

_____

_____ Postcode_____

Email address _____

Tel No(s) _____

Partner's Details (if Joint Membership)

Title _____ Surname_____

Forename(s) _____

Date of Birth (dd/mm/yyyy) _____

	Direct Debit	Non DD
Single Membership (UK & EU)	£20 ☐	£22 ☐
Joint Membership (Partner at the same address)	£25 ☐	£27 ☐

For Young Member and concessionary rates please visit **www.camra.org.uk** or call **01727 867201.**

I wish to join the Campaign for Real Ale, and agree to abide by the Memorandum and Articles of Association

I enclose a cheque for_____

Signed _____ Date_____

Applications will be processed within 21 days

12/10

Campaigning for Pub Goers & Beer Drinkers

Enjoying Real Ale & Pubs

Join CAMRA today – www.camra.org.uk/joinus

Instruction to your Bank or Building Society to pay by Direct Debit

Please fill in the whole form using a ball point pen and send to:
Campaign for Real Ale Ltd, 230 Hatfield Road, St Albans, Herts AL1 4LW

Name and full postal address of your Bank or Building Society

To the Manager _____ Bank or Building Society

Address _____

Postcode _____

Name(s) of Account Holder _____

Branch Sort Code ☐☐☐☐☐☐

Bank or Building Society Account Number ☐☐☐☐☐☐☐☐

Reference ☐☐☐☐☐☐☐☐☐☐☐☐☐☐☐☐☐☐

Service User Number

9 2 6 1 2 9

FOR CAMRA OFFICIAL USE ONLY
This is not part of the instruction to your Bank or Building Society

Membership Number _____

Name _____

Postcode _____

Instructions to your Bank or Building Society
Please pay Campaign For Real Ale Limited Direct Debits from the account detailed on this instruction subject to the safeguards assured by the Direct Debit Guarantee. I understand that this instruction may remain with Campaign for Real Ale Limited and, if so, will be passed electronically to my Bank/Building Society.

Signature(s) _____

Date _____

Banks and Building Societies may not accept Direct Debit Instructions for some types of account.

DIRECT Debit

DIRECT Debit

This Guarantee should be detached and retained by the payer.

The Direct Debit Guarantee

- This Guarantee is offered by all banks and building societies that accept instructions to pay by Direct Debits.
- If there are any changes to the amount, date or frequency of your Direct Debit The Campaign for Real Ale Ltd will notify you 10 working days in advance of your account being debited or as otherwise agreed. If you request The Campaign for Real Ale Ltd to collect a payment, confirmation of the amount and date will be given to you at the time of the request.
- If an error is made in the payment of your Direct Debit by The Campaign for Real Ale Ltd or your bank or building society, you are entitled to a full and immediate refund of the amount paid from your bank or building society.
  - If you receive a refund you are not entitled to, you must pay it back when The Campaign for Real Ale Ltd asks you to.
- You can cancel a Direct Debit at any time by simply contacting your bank or building society. Written confirmation may be required. Please also notify us.

marble that gives the pub its name is in fact Shap granite. It was built in 1888 on the site of a previous 1829 pub as a show house pub for McKenna's brewery and was lit by electricity from the start. The fine barrel-vaulted ceiling and decorative frieze - covered up during alterations in 1954 - were revealed again in the early 1980s. The mosaic sloping floor leads inexorably to the bar and the glazed tile walls add to the splendour of the pub. The back room, which acts as a restaurant, is a much more plain affair, and is a good place to sample the well regarded food. There is also a pleasant beer yard at the rear.

★🏾🐕🎔🍺

by the Boggart Hole Clough brewery, and extended into another stall in 2010 which added some stools by the bar, although seating is generally within the market hall area. Despite this extension it is still a rather small affair, but manages to sell Boggart beers as well as guests including real cider from its five handpumps. As well as draught ales there is a fine selection of bottled British and Continental beers to whet your appetite and whilst it does not sell food, there is plenty of variety available from the surrounding stalls. Although its hours are limited to the market opening times, it is well worth a visit, especially if you have had enough retail therapy in the Arndale.

🍎

MicroBar

Arndale Market, High Street, M4 3AH

☎ 0161 277 9666   (Map: 21)

11-6 Mon-Sat; 12-5 Sun

🌐 boggart-brewery.co.uk

Boggart Rum Porter + seasonal

This interesting and innovative bar was opened by Paradise brewery when the new Arndale opened in 2006. However, during 2009 it was taken over

Millstone

65-67 Thomas Street, M4 1LQ

☎ 0161 839 0213   (Map: 19)

🌐 jwlees.co.uk

10-11 (1 Fri-Sat); 12-10:30 Sun

JW Lees Bitter + seasonal

A lively city centre pub, one which caters mainly for an older clientele, hosting regular singalong evenings performed by the locals; the friendly landlord often mixes and chats with his customers. A former

Wilsons house and acquired by J W Lees in 2004. There are three distinct drinking areas and the large front windows are opened when the weather is clement. It provides inexpensive accommodation and this operation is known as the 'Little Northern Hotel'.

🔔🛏◖

Odd

30-32 Thomas Street, M4 1ER
☎ 0161 833 0070   (Map: 15)
🌐 oddbar.co.uk
11-12 (1 Thu; 1:30 Fri-Sat); 11-12 Sun
Up to four guest ales

This bar opened in 2005 in a converted shop and like several of the new bars in this area has been refurbished and expanded. There are now two public rooms; there's the original ground floor one and a new one upstairs. Each contains a bar with one handpump in the former; and three up in the latter. Both rooms have varied comfortable seating along with bohemian décor, with a relaxed atmosphere and also a free juke box, although the music is not too loud to spoil conversation. There is also a basement cinema showing quirky films. On Wednesday evenings is the quiz night known as 'Quizimodo' and regular DJ slots on Sunday and Thursday evenings. The real ales are usually from local micro breweries, with some decent bottled beers. An unusual chimney stack and pot sits atop the pub.

Smithfield Hotel & Bar

37 Swan Street, M4 5JZ
☎ 0161 839 4424   (Map: 3)
🌐 smithfield-hotel.co.uk
12-12 Mon-Sat; 12-12 Sun
Robinsons Dark Hatters;
Facers Smithfield Bitter +
guests

This is a small and intimate city centre bar that has the atmosphere of a locals' pub. It is situated in the old former Smithfield markets area, which once occupied much of the surroundings, hence its name. On entering by the front street corner door you pass a pool table before reaching the bar on the right, where opposite is a recently created snug with comfy seating. Regular beers are a house bitter brewed by Facer's along with a couple of others from the Robinsons' stable, with the remaining handpumps providing an ever changing range of beers from breweries far and wide. In the rear drinking area there is a large television for showing sport and reasonably priced room only accommodation is available.

🛏♣

Soup Kitchen

31-33 Spear Street, M1 1DF
☎ 0161 236 5100   (Map: 20)
🌐 soup-kitchen.co.uk
11-7 (1 Thu-Sat); 11-7 Sun
Up to two guest ales

A pleasant bar and bistro serving everything you would expect from a refectory style canteen. Soups, snacks, main meals and up to two real ales are available and there is also a variety of British and Continental bottled beers too. A downstairs room opened in 2011, providing more room for what was a not very large bar. One of the unusual features is the presence of 'Good Grief', an independent small press and fanzine shop: (goodgriefshop.blogspot.com). ✿◖

TV21

10 Thomas Street, M4 1DH
☎ 0161 819 2221   (Map: 13)
🌐 tv21manchester.com
4-1; 12-1 Tue-Thu; (3 Fri-Sat); 12-1 Sun
Moorhouse's Premier Bitter

A television, film and arts themed venue, recently converted to real ale in 2011. A large metal 'alien' watches over the entrance and there are other film memorabilia items inside. The most noticeable of these is the Space Shuttle snug which is now probably the only operational one left. Food is available until 9 pm daily and there is a quiz night on a Wednesday, supplemented by other occasional special events including film and band nights. ✿◖

Unicorn

26 Church Street, M4 1PN
☎ 0161 834 8854   (Map: 23)
11:30-11 Mon-Sat; 12-10 Sun
Copper Dragon Challenger, Golden Pippin + guests

This multi-roomed pub is usually a very busy affair during the day, populated with a lively band of regulars who can be boisterous but friendly, but generally it is not as busy in the evenings. A large central bar services a narrow lounge and also a lobby that leads to a large lounge off to the right. A small back room has a television and an interesting collection of naval themed pictures, with the bar and rooms consisting of carefully preserved light oak panelling. Apparently in former times, this was the meeting place of the famed Honourable Order of Bass Drinkers.

Wheatsheaf

30 Oak Street, M4 5JE
☎ 0161 833 9445   (Map: 11)
🌐 marstonspubcompany.co.uk
12-12 Mon-Sat; 12-10:30 Sun
Marston's Pedigree

A large pub and one which used to serve the old Smithfield markets area, but is now hidden within the small housing estate that developed over much of the area. It has a large bar along the back wall in the middle of the pub which was altered in the 1990s. While it is essentially open plan the layout gives the feel of four separate drinking areas. It started selling real ale again in early 2010, after a lengthy absence and has re-established itself in the real ale fold quite comfortably. Regular live music evenings are provided by a keyboardist. It sits across the road from the Manchester Craft and Design Centre, which is housed in the old retail fish market.

🏚️🍺♣

Other Pubs and Bars in This Area

Apotheca
17 Thomas Street, M4 1EU
☎ 0161 834 9411 (Map: A)
Bar Centro
74 Tib Street, M4 1LG (Map: B)
Barcelona
6 Hilton Street, M4 1NB
☎ 0161 839 7117 (Map: C)
Blackdog Ballroom
Church Street, M1 1JG
☎ 0161 839 0664 (Map: D)

Cord
8 Dorsey Street, M4 1LU
☎ 0161 832 9494 (Map: E)
Dry Bar
28 Oldham Street, M1 1JN
☎ 0161 236 9840 (Map: F)
Hula
11a Stevenson Square, M1 1DB
☎ 0161 228 7421 (Map: G)
Joes Bar
4 Oldham Street, M1 1JQ
☎ 0161 228 0517 (Map: H)
Keko Moku
100-102 High Street, M4 1HP
☎ 0161 832 6568 (Map: I)
Night & Day
26 Oldham Street, M1 1JN
☎ 0161 236 1822 (Map: J)
Noho
Stevenson Square, M1 1FB
☎ 0161 236 5381 (Map: K)
Northern
56 Tib Street, M4 1LW
☎ 0161 835 2548 (Map: L)
Simple
38-40 Tib Street, M4 1LA
☎ 0161 832 8764 (Map: M)
Simple at the Light
20 Church Street, M4 1PN
☎ 0871 231 775 (Map: N)
Socio Rehab
108 High Street, M4 1HQ
☎ 0161 832 4529 (Map: O)
Thomas Street Bar & Restaurant
49-51 Thomas Street, M4 1NA
☎ 0161 839 7033 (Map: P)
Trof
6-8 Thomas Street, M4 1EU
☎ 0161 833 3197 (Map: Q)
Walrus
78-88 High Street, M4 1ES
☎ 0161 828 8700 (Map: R)
Wave Bar (Sasha)
Tib Street, M4 1SH
☎ 0161 228 1234 (Map: S)

Piccadilly and The Village

Piccadilly Gardens

Piccadilly Station, Manchester's main inter-city rail station is located to the south east of the city. North of it are the main Piccadilly Gardens bus station and Manchester Central coach station at Chorlton Street. The area to the south of the coach station centring on Canal Street is Manchester's 'Gay Village', popular with young revellers, hen and stag nights but home to a wide variety of pubs and bars serving all sections of the community. Portland Street is lined by many of Manchester's oldest and largest hotels. To the very south of the area is Manchester University's North Campus.

Attractions in This Area Include

Piccadilly Station
Piccadilly Gardens
Manchester Central Coach Station
Canal Street

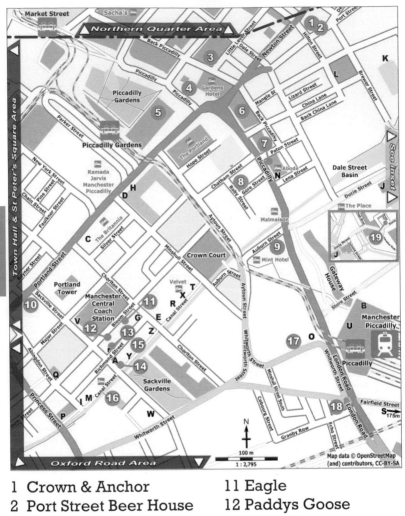

1 Crown & Anchor
2 Port Street Beer House
3 Mother Mac's
4 Wetherspoons
5 Kro Piccadilly
6 Piccadilly Tavern
7 B Lounge @ The Brunswick
8 Waldorf
9 City Café & Bars (Mint Hotel)
10 Yates's
11 Eagle
12 Paddys Goose
13 Molly House
14 Rembrandt / Rem Bar
15 Crunch
16 Eden
17 Outpost
18 Bulls Head
19 Jolly Angler

B Lounge @ The Brunswick

97 Piccadilly, M1 2DB
☎ 0161 236 4161   (Map: 7)
⊕ blounge.co.uk/piccadilly.htm
9-12 Mon-Sat; 10-11 Sun
Theakston Best Bitter,

Thwaites Bomber + guest

This is the former Brunswick, now under the same management as its counterpart, the B-Lounge @ The Bridge. On entering the pub via a couple of steps the bar with its three handpumps is before you. To the left is a small room with a large picture covering the majority of one wall, and these are either cream painted or bare brick with some mirrors and occasional pictures. To the right of the bar is the main lounge area and to the rear is a raised area on the right with a smaller area to the left. It is all smart seating with comfy chairs and sofas and there is also a large outside seating area which encompasses the pavement, segregated from what is a busy thoroughfare. ✿WiFi

Bulls Head

84 London Road, M1 2PN
☎ 0161 236 1724   (Map: 18)
11:30-11 Mon-Sat; 12-10:30 Sun
Banks's Original, Jennings

Cumberland + guests

Situated across the road from the rear entrance to Piccadilly rail station, this ornately painted Victorian exterior attracts both travellers and a faithful band of regulars. While the interior is basically open-plan it nevertheless manages to

generate the atmosphere of cosy intimacy that you might expect to find in a more suburban location. Run with superb professionalism across the board, it never disappoints and is a beacon for quality. Evidence of this is in the numerous awards from both CAMRA and trade bodies received in recent years for the quality of their beer and pub. The guest beers are usually from the Marston's stable but beer festivals and other promotions see other brewers' products making an appearance. Evening food is served from 5.30 pm to 8.30 pm on Mondays to Thursdays. Q🕐&🚃(M1,M3)

City Café & Bars (Mint Hotel)

1 Auburn Street, M1 3DG
☎ 0161 242 1030   (Map: 9)
⊕ minthotel.com/manchester
12-11 Mon-Sat; 12-11 Sun
Harviestoun Bitter & Twisted,

Schiehallion

Incorporating Blue Bar and the Piccadilly Lounge and housed inside the Mint Hotel. The former is a small, intimate and stylish pre-dinner drinks bar with dark blue decor, furnishings and sultry blue lighting making it a cosy and quiet venue that can seat approximately 15-20 people.

Offering an extensive drinks menu of spirits, wines and cocktails, with a varied bottled beer selection and two draught beers are available which are subject to seasonal change, served from a European-style tap. Both bars boast an excellent comprehensive whisky library which is arranged by region. The latter is located at the front of the hotel by the reception and is larger, busier and more brightly-lit than the other. It has the same drinks menu and although both bars are open to non-residents, it has more regular non-resident customers. Also offers hot and cold bar meals, snacks and afternoon teas and a fresh serving of mixed warm beer nuts is served with every drinks order. Average four-star hotel bar prices for both drinks and bar meals reflected by the quality of its surroundings and service.

⛵✿⌂◖⅃♿☒(M1,M3)

Crown & Anchor

41 Hilton Street, M1 2EE
☎ 0161 228 1142　　(Map: 1)
12-11 (12 Fri-Sat); 12-11 Sun
Caledonian Deuchars IPA,
Timothy Taylor Landlord +
guest

The original interior was ripped out in the 1960s creating the layout that exists today. This was refurbished in 2011 with silver-grey walls, pine flooring and charcoal carpeted areas giving it a more up market feel. There are normally three real ales along with Westons Scrumpy cider available in this former 'Beer Engine' street corner pub. There is a separate pool room at the rear and an attractive roof terrace for outdoor drinking. It looks like the pub's fortunes might be on the up again after a spell of indifference. There has been a pub here for a long time, being licensed before 1800. In the 1930s nearby Stevenson Square was used for public speaking and at the end of the day the speakers would reconvene to this pub, no doubt putting the world to rights.

✿⌂◖♣♥

Crunch

10 Canal Street, M1 3EZ
☎ 0161 236 0446　　(Map: 15)
🌐 crunchbar.co.uk
12-2:30 (4.30 Fri-Sat); 12-2.30 Sun
Black Sheep Best Bitter

Modern bar with large open spaces, set on two levels (upstairs is the Upper Crunch). Side booths provide privacy and comfort, yet in general this is a stand-up drinks bar with plenty of dance space. It is great to see a bar such as this trying out cask ale.

✿☒(M1,M3)

Eagle

15 Bloom Street, M1 3HZ
☎ 0161 228 6669   (Map: 11)
🌐 eaglemanchester.com
5-3 (4 Fri; 5 Sat); 5-3 Sun
Wells & Youngs Eagle IPA

Complementing Manchester's industrial history, with a nod towards a plush Victorian style, this downstairs bar has behind it the Black Eagle, a club with a dance area. There is quite a small L-shaped space with a bright bar and a cosy black-furnished lounge room that lies behind. The main room lighting is dim, yet colour comes from the red furnishings matched with tables fashioned from travel chests. Please note the Eagle operates as a male members-only bar (to enquire about membership, email: info@eaglemanchester.com). A new venture, the Richmond Tea House is planned to open in August 2011 in the space above the Eagle. This will be open to all, with planned opening hours of 11 am until 11 pm daily.
♿🍴(M1,M3)

Eden

3 Brazil Street, M1 3PW
☎ 0161 237 9852   (Map: 13)
🌐 edenbar.co.uk
11:30-11 (2 Fri-Sat); 11:30-11 Sun
Black Sheep Best Bitter

This is a striking bar-restaurant that exists in two parts, two mediums even. The first part you encounter is the water-borne former barge and terrace that operates as an alfresco drinking and dining location on the Rochdale Canal. Then you enter the building itself to a smart interior where food has a focus. Relaxing sofas lead onto a lower bar area with more formal tables set out. Meals served 12 pm until 10 pm.
🌭🍴🍺(M1,M3)

Jolly Angler

47 Ducie Street, M1 2JW
☎ 0161 236 5307   (Map: 19)
🌐 hydesbrewery.co.uk
12-2 & 5:30-11; 12-11 Sat; 2-4; 8-11 Sun
Hydes Original + seasonal

The pub was built in 1854 on land previously occupied by the Good Samaritan Temperance Hall! Not an architectural gem but it is a small street corner local, of a type once common, but now rare. A back corner bar serves two distinct drinking areas that used to be separate rooms. The pub has been run by the same family for about 27 years and Irish music features along with a regular folk night. It gets busy on live music nights and when Manchester City play football at their nearby stadium. Weekday lunchtime hours can vary according to the level of trade. It is a friendly pub of character and has its fair share of characters.

🏚🍴(M1,M2)

Kro Piccadilly

1 Piccadilly Gardens, M1 1RG
☎ 0161 244 5765   (Map: 5)
🌐 kro.co.uk
8-11 (9-11 Fri; 12:30 Sat); 9-11 Sun
Marstons EPA, Thwaites
Wainwright + guest

The most prestigious of the Danish Kro chain of pubs and bars (see also the entry below for Kro2) and occupies part of the ground floor of One Piccadilly Gardens. Inside, the predominance of concrete and glass can make for a noisy environment, what with both music and conversation, making the latter very difficult. This is a stylish setup though

that caters equally well for those dining (full Danish menu), as it does for those just here for a drink. Can get extremely busy on Friday evenings especially with the after-work crowd and at weekends. If the weather is good, the outside tables are almost impossible to sit at. The food is available all day whilst the beer selection tends to vary from time to time, with some interesting foreign bottles rounding it all off.

🐾◐♿🍴(M1,M3)

Molly House

26 Richmond Street, M1 3NB
☎ 0161 237 9329   (Map: 13)
🌐 themollyhouse.com
12-12 (1 Thu; 2 Fri-Sat); 12-1 Sun
Beartown Black Bear +
seasonals

A brand new bar and café, it opened in December 2010 in a former worsted tailors shop that may well be starting a new movement in the village. Not just a bar, it does 20 different teas, specialist coffees, and high-end spirits. The name derives from the London molly houses of the Victorian period. It is set on two levels, its decor described as post-Victorian decadent and shabby chic and on the ground floor, 'The Tea Room' has the cask ale bar together with the food servery. Intended as a stand-up drinking space, furnishings here are spartan, whilst upstairs in the 'The Bordello', the decor and lighting is more intimate. This floor has a bar too, with sofas and a fireplace adding warmth. An outside smoking and

drinking veranda finishes the impressive package. Food service is from 12 pm until 8 pm and is of the lite-bite variety and there is a real cider from Westons.
◑🍎🚌(M1,M3)

Mother Mac's

33 Back Piccadilly, M1 1HP
☎ 0161 236 1507 (Map: 3)
11:30-11:30 Mon-Sat; 11:30-11 Sun
Hydes Original

This is a small one roomed back street pub which caters for a mature clientele. It is a friendly place and has been run by the same landlady for 26 years. The one handpump on the bar that distributes cask ale from Hydes' oversees the L-shaped room, with its several separate fixed seating areas. A long time ago it was known as the Wellington but was renamed in memory of Norah McLellan, a former long serving landlady.
♣

Outpost

6 Whitworth Street, M1 3QW
☎ 0161 236 5400 (Map: 17)
🌐 legendsmanchester.com
12-11 (12 Fri & Sat); 12-11 Sun
Fullers London Pride, Shaws Golden Globe

A comfortable, smallish sub-basement bar that also acts as a feeder or an annexe to the Legends club, which is next door. The front room has a long bar with mirrored-ceiling work whilst at the rear is large room used for dancing and entertainment; it also houses a stage. A popular happy-hour operates until 7 pm attracting a mixed crowd, plus it gets busy at weekends. A very handy stop -off if you have a lengthy wait for a train at Piccadilly rail station.
❀🚌(M1,M3)

Paddys Goose

29 Bloom Street, M1 3JE
☎ 0161 236 1246 (Map: 12)
12-11 (12 Wed-Fri; 12:30 Sat); 12-12 Sun
Robinsons Unicorn, Wells & Youngs Bombardier

A pub of the more traditional sort and in which wood and paint, rather than glass and chrome reign supreme and seats are there for the taking. The decor appears to almost be

a throwback to its old Magic Pub Company days. It is the sort of pub where you might say all human life is here. The interesting decor includes mirrors, pictures and general stuff including a whisky box collection. It is handy for Manchester's Central Coach Station, whilst food service is 12 pm until 6.30 pm.

🚌(M1,M3)

Piccadilly

71-73 Piccadilly, M1 2BS
☎ 0161 237 0201 (Map: 6)
8-11 (12 Fri; 1 Sat); 9-11 Sun
Up to three guest ales

A large split-level pub which has left a somewhat varied past well behind it. It is now a welcoming stop between Piccadilly bus, rail and tram stations. Marston's EPA alternates with John Smith's cask, with a keen manager who is committed to real ale, ensures the two guests which supplement these are often interesting ones. The bar is in the front of the pub at the lower level whilst a large raised area is at the rear. Good value food is served until 9.30 pm and is very busy on football match days due to the proximity of the transport termini.

◖🚌(M1,M3)

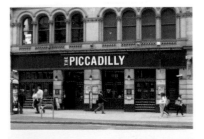

Port Street Beer House

39-41 Port Street, M1 2EQ
☎ 0161 237 9949 (Map: 2)
🌐 portstreetbeerhouse.co.uk
4-12; 12-1 Sat; 12-12 Sun
Up to seven guest ales

A recently opened bar in a back street, specialising in craft beers from all over the world. There are seven handpumps and a wide selection of other draught beers and bottled beers available, mostly from the USA. Beer menus are available to help you choose your tipple; the bar is on the ground floor, while the toilets are on the first, along with additional seating. The décor is minimalist but smart and there is also a beer garden at the rear. A rather expensive experience, it has nevertheless become very popular and finding a seat can be difficult at busy times. The staff is usually knowledgeable about the beers and regular beer tasting events are held. It was converted from a shop that for just a few years in the 1860s had been a licensed beer house called the 'Farmers Boy' which makes a 150 year gap between serving pints. This current venture is destined to last a little longer.
❀WiFi

Rembrandt / Rem Bar

33 Sackville Street, M1 3LZ
☎ 0161 236 1311 (Map: 14)
🌐 rembar.co.uk
12-12 (1 Thu; 3 Fri-Sat); 12-12 Sun
JW Lees Coronation St Ale

Two bars contained inside one building and formerly the

Rembrandt. The lower Rem Bar has recently been refurbished to a high standard - all black and silver decor with tasteful use of a military boot motif in the logo and artefacts in and around the bar. There isn't much furniture, so the emphasis is on vertical drinking and this bar is another of the men-only vocation. The upstairs area, comprising of the Belinda Scandal showbar, is accessed from the Sackville Street entrance and accepts both sexes, however, this is only open in the evening, being a more plush affair. There is no cask ale in this bar.

🕸🚪👤♿🚌(M1,M3)

ceiling. Mainly open plan (which seems to amplify the piped music), screened-off seating areas, some with sofas, affording some privacy to those wishing it. It can become quite busy when televised football is being shown.

🕸🍴🚌(M1,M3)

Waldorf

12 Gore Street, M1 3AQ
☎ 0161 228 3269　　(Map: 8)
11-11 Mon-Sat; 12-10:30 Sun
Caledonian Deuchars IPA,
Timothy Taylor Landlord

Situated just off the bustling Piccadilly thoroughfare, this old but attractive building stands quietly tucked away amid the modern office blocks to lure the passers-by in. The interior though is of more modern times, yet it gives a feeling of provenance with wainscoted walls and a match-boarded

Wetherspoons

49 Piccadilly, M1 2AP
☎ 0161 236 9206　　(Map: 4)
🌐 jdwetherspoon.co.uk
7-11 (11:30 Wed-Sat); 7-11 Sun
Greene King Abbot Ale,
Ruddles + guests

While JD Wetherspoons refer to this pub as The Manchester and County, there is no apparent reference to this outside the pub itself. It is a very busy open plan pub with a long bar down the left hand side and a raised area to the rear. There's a much improved selection of guest ales with the arrival of a new manager, and all the usual food and drinks offers are available. It couldn't be better situated for public transport with buses, trains and trams all nearby. There is ground level access and facilities for wheelchair users.

🍴♿👤🚌(M1,M3)

Piccadilly

Yates's

49 Portland Street, M1 3LD
☎ 0161 228 0162   (Map: 10)
🌐 weareyates.co.uk/manchester
10-12 (1 Thu; 2 Fri-Sat); 10-12 Sun

Yates House Best Bitter, Wells & Youngs Bombardier

You enter into a large open space with a raised alcove area to the right leading to an outside seating and smoking patio, enclosed by a fence. A long curved bar sits along the back wall with the decor being dark wood panelling and strip flooring with a purple carpet in the raised area. There is a good range of food, which is very competitively priced as is the wine. The toilets are a trek up four flights of stairs but there is a disabled one and a baby change facility on the ground floor. Similar in many ways to their rival Wetherspoon's, but not so cluttered with menus, so giving equal balance between wet trade and food. A fairly noisy place, with low background music and television screens.
&⦿◑&🚆(M1,M3)

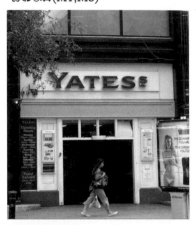

Other Pubs and Bars in This Area

Baa Bar
27 Sackville Street, M1 3LZ
☎ 0161 247 7997   (Map: A)
Balcony Bar
Mezzanine, Piccadilly Station, M1 2BN
☎ 0161 236 3613   (Map: B)
Bar Rogue / Wave
Britannia Hotel, 35 Portland Street, M1 3LA
☎ 0161 228 7007   (Map: C)
Blue Parrot
11 Portland Street, M1 3HU
☎ 0161 236 8359   (Map: D)
Churchills
37 Chorlton Street, M1 3HN
☎ 0161 236 5529   (Map: E)
Company Bar
28 Richmond Street, M1 3NB
☎ 0161 237 9329   (Map: F)
Coyotes
14 Chorlton Street, M1 3HW
☎ 0161 236 4007   (Map: G)
Edwards / Missoula
11 Westminster House, Portland Street, M1 3HU
☎ 0161 237 0631   (Map: H)
G-A-Y
48 Canal Street, M1 3ND
☎ 0161 228 6200   (Map: I)
Green
Ducie Wharf, 26 Ducie Street, M1 2DQ
☎ 0161 228 0681   (Map: J)
Jacksons Retro Bar
Jackson's Warehouse, 20 Tariff Street, M1 2FJ
☎ 0161 228 2677   (Map: K)
Lammars
Fourways House, 57 Hilton Street, M1 2EJ
☎ 0161 237 9058   (Map: L)
Manto
46 Canal Street, M1 3WD
☎ 0161 236 2667   (Map: M)

MC Bar & Grill (Abode hotel)
107 Piccadilly, M1 2DB
☎ 0161 200 5665   (Map: N)
Monroe's
38 London Road, M1 2PF
☎ 0161 236 0564   (Map: O)
New Union
111 Princess Street, M1 6JB
☎ 0161 228 1492   (Map: P)
New York, New York
94 Bloom Street, M1 3LY
☎ 0161 236 6556   (Map: Q)
Queer
4 Canal Street, M1 3HE
☎ 0161 228 1360   (Map: R)
Star & Garter
18-20 Fairfield Street, M1 2QF
☎ 0161 273 6726   (Map: S)
Taurus
1 Canal Street, M1 3HE
☎ 0161 236 4593   (Map: T)
Terrace Sports Bar
Mezzanine, Piccadilly Station, M1 2BN
☎ 0161 236 7280   (Map: U)
Thompson Arms
23 Sackville Street, M1 3LZ
☎ 0161 228 3012   (Map: V)
Tribeca / Bed
50 Sackville Street, M1 3WF
☎ 0161 236 8300   (Map: W)
Velvet
2 Canal Street, M1 3HE
☎ 0161 236 9003   (Map: X)
Via
28-30 Canal Street, M1 3EZ
☎ 0161 236 6523   (Map: Y)
View
40 Chorlton Street, M1 3HW
☎ 0161 236 9033   (Map: Z)

Piccadilly

CAMRA encourages responsible drinking. Please see drinkaware.co.uk for further details

Manchester in Three Days

Manchester's city centre is unique in that it incorporates three different branches of CAMRA (the Campaign for Real Ale) and also fits quite adequately into three main sections and areas to visit, but not necessarily in conjunction with the branch areas. They make an ideal pub crawl, either for walking or using public transport. Here are some of the highlights.

Day one: The first and one of the most well known areas of these is the Northern Quarter. Extending northwards, this normally incorporates the **Marble Arch Inn,** which is the farthest point and then the **Angel Pub** (formerly the revered Beer House), a short distance away. It is then possible to saunter around and visit the **Smithfield Hotel & Bar, Bar Fringe, Crown & Kettle** and the **Castle Hotel.** To finish off (or begin in reverse) the **Hare & Hounds** is on CAMRA's National Inventory (NI) of historic pubs. This is opposite the Shudehill Interchange for buses and the Shudehill tram stop. If you have the time or the inclination, there are numerous other bars around this area to pass the time away

Day two: Our second area features the former industrial and historical sites around the Deansgate-Castlefield streets. The **Knott** sits conveniently opposite Deansgate railway station and the Deansgate-Castlefield tram stop. From here there is **Cask,** the **White Lion,** and the **Ox** (which styles itself as a gastro-pub); a short distance away is another NI classic in the 200 year old **Briton's Protection** then a short walk along the same street to the **Rain Bar,** one of J W Lees' flagship pubs. Yet another NI pub beckons as across the road is the **Peveril Of The Peak,** run for 40 years by the same landlady. This is an easy walk and can be continued up to Oxford Road (where there is another railway station) taking in theatreland and one or two other bars here.

Day Three: The third and final foray centres upon Manchester's architectural history, around St Peter's Square, (yet another tram stop here), the Town Hall and Portland Street areas. The Central Library imposes itself on St Peter's Square and by the side of the striking gothic Town Hall is the **Waterhouse.** Next door is the **City Arms** and also the **Vine Inn.** Others in this locale include the **Old Monkey, Circus Tavern** and **Grey Horse Inn,** three pubs all from different breweries. Around the corner from these is the stunning Chinese Arch, a tribute to the Chinese community, and a 'must see' for any new visitor. Close by is the **Seven Oaks** and a short stroll towards the Piccadilly area with three tram stops and a bus station is the **Bank** housed in a wonderful building which incorporates the Portico Library.

See the *Inn Sight of Manchester's History* article for further information regarding the historical buildings of Manchester.

Oxford Road

The Palace Theatre and the Palace Hotel

Oxford Road (with its northern extension Oxford Street connecting to St Peter's Square) is the main road route into the city from the south. The area also has its own rail station primarily serving destinations to the east and west. As the road runs through the heart of Manchester University, Manchester Metropolitan University and the Royal Northern College of Music, the area is popular with Manchester's 80,000+ student population. To the south Oxford Road becomes Wilmslow Road - see section 9.

Attractions in This Area Include

Oxford Road Station
Palace Theatre
Cornerhouse Arts Centre
Manchester Metropolitan University

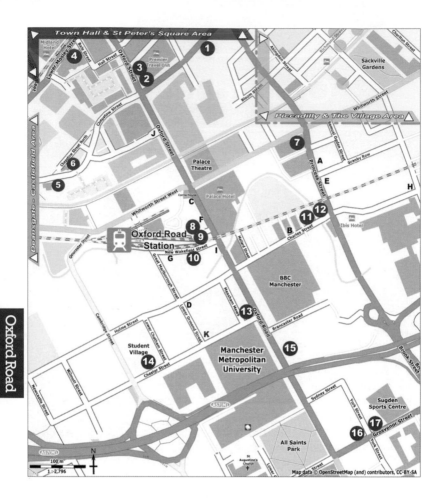

1	Fab Café	10	Font
2	Paramount	11	Lass O'Gowrie
3	Alibi	12	Joshua Brooks
4	Table Table	13	Odder
5	Rain Bar	14	Courtyard
6	Peveril of the Peak	15	Kro2
7	O'Sheas	16	Pub / Zoo
8	Salisbury Hotel	17	Sandbar
9	Thirsty Scholar		

Alibi

31 Oxford Street, M1 4BH
☎ 0161 237 5051 (Map: 3)
🌐 thealibimanchester.co.uk
8-12 Mon-Sat; (2 Fri); 8-12 Sun
Thwaites Wainwright, Wells &
Youngs Bombardier + guests

A recent convert to cask beer under its keen new management, providing a comfortable and sophisticated city centre watering hole. A complete overhaul has seen the bar repositioned and aimed at a slightly older clientele. The new look has seen the interior split up in eclectic fashion with a number of different drinking areas, subdued lighting and a mix and match collection of comfortable seating; there is even an upstairs VIP area which can be hired for private gatherings. The guest beers come from regional and micro breweries (Denton's Hornbeam Brewery often features) and there are also occasional beer festivals. Good value food is served every day from 8 am until 9 pm.
◑&🍴🚃(M1,M3)

Courtyard

2 Chester Street, M1 5SH
☎ 07834 666137 (Map: 14)
11-1 (2 Fri-Sat); 12-12 Sun
Black Sheep Best Bitter,
Hydes Finest

Situated on the ground floor of the Student Village accommodation building, but is open to all. Food and drink prices are some of the cheapest in the area, with evenings very busy, especially Friday and Saturday nights when students

congregate, but at other times this can be a very pleasant place for a quite drink or a bite to eat. Popular for sports fans are the televisions with up to four separate games being shown at any one time. There are three pool tables plus table football and pinball. The pool and table football games along with the jukebox are free until 8 pm (3 pm on Saturdays and Sundays). To the rear is a large covered area complete with two television screens.
🕸◑&♣🍴

Fab Café

109 Portland Street, M1 6DN
☎ 0161 212 2997 (Map: 1)
🌐 fabcafe.co.uk
4:30-2 Mon-Sat; 5-1 Sun
Black Sheep Best Bitter

Set in a cellar, the entrance from street level is down a set of steps and through silver double doors. A single large dimly-lit space greets you, with the bar on the right. You may notice that almost every bit of wall space is covered in posters and portraits of various actors; the ceiling gets the treatment too, with plenty of spaceship models hanging from it. This was the city's first cult-TV and Sci-Fi theme bar after all, becoming a cult attraction in itself. Hence you find a mock-up of the

Oxford Road

starship Enterprise's bridge area (used as a podium for the DJ), whilst next to this is a forlorn looking Dalek and K-9 keeps a welcome guard on the doorway. Display cabinets at either end of the bar are full of Sci-Fi toys and memorabilia; board games are available to play with too. If pinball is your game, one of the city's few machines is located here. A varied clientele makes this an engaging place to stop awhile and there is a quiz held every Wednesday evening, whilst food is served daily except Sundays, between 4.30 pm and 9 pm (7.30 pm Fridays and Saturdays). Ask the staff if you wish to use the Wi-Fi.

❋♣🚆(M1,M3)WiFi

Font

7-9 New Wakefield Street, M1 5NP

☎ 0161 236 0944   (Map: 10)
🌐 fontbar.com
11-1 Mon-Sat; 11-12:30 Sun
Up to two guest ales

At first glance, an uncompromising site, yet within there's a funky, eclectic multi-level space. Fashioned over two levels (the upper level bar is the only one that serves real

ale, the basement bar doesn't), good use is made of differing decor, furniture and lighting to create different moods. Ideal for meeting up with friends or drinking alone, they have two handpumps with rotating guest beers, often from unusual breweries. Aimed at a studenty, youthful clientele, it offers a selection of cocktails and an excellent British themed food menu until 8 pm. Currently there is discount for card carrying CAMRA members on real ales and real ciders.

❋♿🚆(M2)WiFi

Joshua Brooks

106 Princess Street, M1 6NG
☎ 0161 273 7336   (Map: 12)
🌐 joshuabrooks.co.uk
11-12 (12-2 Fri-Sat); 12-12 Sun
Up to five guest ales

Wedged beside the industrial heritage of the Oxford Rd railway viaduct and the River Medlock, indeed the seldom seen river can be viewed from a pleasant balcony. This is a sister pub to the Deansgate and Thirsty Scholar, it is a smart, modern yet traditional bar that is both relaxing and busy. Fixed seating sits down one side, with dining furniture and Chesterfield sofas in front of the bar. Plenty of doors on the opposite side of the room give you access to that river view, whilst telly-watchers are catered for in large-screen style (usually muted). Five handpulls serve a good mix of micro-brewery sourced ales. Food is served daily 11-7 (5 Sat-Sun)

❋❋❋🚆(M1,M3)

Kro2

Oxford House, Oxford Road, M1 7ED
☎ 0161 236 1048   (Map: 15)
⊕ kro.co.uk
8:30-12 Mon-Sat; 9:30-11 Sun
***Thwaites Wainwright, Wells &
Youngs Bombardier + guests***

A conversion of the ground floor of a former office building and you can just imagine the foyer of a 1960s building with a bar sited in the middle of it. Full-height glazing lets the natural light flood into this innovative modern space. Set back from the busy Oxford Road, with outside tables to the front, whilst much covered and heated seating is to the side of this in the shadow of the snaking, concrete viaduct that is the Mancunian Way. The inside meanwhile accommodates diners to the left, whilst the remainder is for the drinkers. As this is a Danish pub (and sister pub to Kro Piccadilly), the menu features many tasty specialities from that nation. Drinkers are not left out though as beer festivals are held, typically twice a year, whilst the normal cask range varies weekly supplemented by Westons cider or a guest, and a bottled beer range that covers the world. Food is served

throughout the day, every day of the week.
🛇🕭◖♿♨🚌(M2)

Lass O'Gowrie

36 Charles Street, M1 7DB
☎ 0161 273 6932   (Map: 11)
⊕ thelass.co.uk
12-12 (10-12 Sat); 10-12 Sun
Black Sheep Best Bitter + guests

From the outside a splendid

Victorian glazed tiled building; once inside the traditionalism changes. Gas lamps (no longer working), walls festooned with northern performing arts ephemera and very popular with students in term time, it can be rather lacking vibrancy during academic breaks, so much so that there is a 'Fringe Festival' throughout July. '70s and '80s pub arcade game machines are dotted about along with some nostalgic micro computer murals on the walls. Ten handpulls adorn the bar, of which three are for beers of the landlord's choosing. There is a snug tucked away at the back for small informal gatherings and a larger function room upstairs caters for up to 40 people. Note the clever use of decking built over the River Medlock to create a smoking balcony opened by comedian and pub regular Johnny Vegas, with a plaque on the wall to mark the event.

🐾◑♣

Odder

14 Oxford Road, M1 5QA
☎ 0161 238 9132 (Map: 13)
🌐 odderbar.co.uk
12-12 (1 Thu; 2 Fri-Sat); 12-12 Sun
Up to three guest ales

This larger sibling to the Northern Quarter's Odd bar is spread over two floors, although the spacious upstairs bar only opens evenings. The decor is quirky, from the buffalo head above the door to a wall covered in clocks. There is a good range of drinks and an extensive food menu is served all day including breakfasts and brunches (until 4 pm), pizzas, sandwiches and favourites like burgers and fish and chips. Between Wednesdays to Sundays, Odder turns into part bar, part club, with a selection of DJs playing different styles of music each night from folk to indie, pop to hip-hop. While the focus for the club nights is the upstairs bar, it can be loud in both.

🛏🐾◑ WiFi

O'Sheas

80 Princess Street, M1 6NF
☎ 0161 236 3906 (Map: 7)
12-11 Mon-Sat; 12-10:30 Sun
Black Sheep Best Bitter

An Irish pub housed in an old William & Glynn's bank yet despite that pedigree, this L-shaped bar is somewhat basic, almost like a 1970s works canteen with red painted woodwork, half-panelling on the walls, bench seating and wood flooring. On the walls is the usual Irish bric-a-brac expected of an 'Irish' theme bar. Round the corner from the entrance is a stage area that hosts regular live music, and a pool table. Irish TV sports are shown via RTE (Radío Teilifís Éireann), the Irish broadcasting company.

♣🖵(M1,M3)

Paramount

33-35 Oxford Street, M1 4BH
☎ 0161 233 1820 (Map: 2)
🌐 jdwetherspoon.co.uk
9-12 (1 Fri-Sat); 9-12 Sun
Elland Paramount Porter,
Greene King Abbot Ale +
guests

So named because of its location in Manchester's old theatre-land, this large and extremely popular Wetherspoon's pub has a very lively, yet always controlled atmosphere. However, what really sets it apart is the enthusiasm of the team here for their wide and interesting range of cask beers. Old photos of now closed theatres and cinemas adorn the walls but it is still very handy for many modern day venues, including Manchester Central Conference Centre, the Palace Theatre and the Bridgewater Hall.

◑&♿☕🚲(M1,M3)

Peveril Of The Peak

127 Great Bridgewater Street, M1 5JQ
☎ 0161 236 6364　　(Map: 6)
12-3 & 5-11 Mon-Fri; 5-11 Sat; 5-10:30 Sun
Caledonian Deuchars IPA,
Copper Dragon Golden Pippin
+ guests

A Manchester institution and a straightforward drinkers' pub, run by the same management since 1971. Grade II listed and on CAMRA's National Inventory of Historic Pub Interiors for many original features, including the famous green, yellow and cream tiled exterior that dates back to 1900. Internally there are three rooms plus a large drinking lobby and in the main bar there is a selection of photos of famous visitors alongside many awards won by the pub. The rear room has a Victorian cast iron fireplace with marble surrounds, above which is a large etched mirror presented by CAMRA to commemorate the 40th anniversary of landlady Nancy Swannick.

★🎵Q🌭◑♣🚲(M2)

Pub / Zoo

126 Grosvenor Street, M1 7HL
☎ 0161 274 4743　　(Map: 16)
11-12 (2 Thu; 1 Fri-Sat); 12-12 Sun
Greene King, Old Speckled Hen,
Marston's Pedigree + guest

This former plumbers merchants started life as an Irish bar about 20 years ago. Some remnants of that remain on the left of the pub with small compartments and an attractive snug at the back. The rest of the pub is largely open plan but all is furnished with a mix and match style which give the place a comfortable lived-in feel and the table football is an unusual find. Food is served 11 am until 10 pm in university term time, reducing to 12 pm until 9 pm in the summer months. The opening hours may also be curtailed when the students are away. The beer range may vary between standard offerings from regional brewers.

🌭◑🚲

Oxford Road

Rain Bar

80 Great Bridgewater Street, M1 5JG
☎ 0161 235 6500   (Map: 5)
🌐 rain-bar.co.uk
12-11 (12 Fri-Sat); 12-8 Sun
(seasonal)
JW Lees Bitter + seasonals

Occupying a prime location on the Rochdale Canal, this former umbrella factory was converted into brewer JW Lees' flagship pub in the 90s and remains one of the few pubs of theirs where the full cask ale range is served. The ground floor area curves around three sides of the large bar with lots of dark wood and a variety of raised and sunken areas giving a traditional feel. The large patio area alongside the canal is one of the largest outdoor drinking areas in the city and can get very busy during summer. Pub food is served until 8 pm on weekdays and until 6 pm at weekends and there are two function rooms available for hire upstairs.
🏨🍴🕍♿WiFi

Oxford Road

Salisbury Hotel

2 Wakefield Street, M1 5NE
☎ 0161 236 5590   (Map: 8)
12-1 (2 Fri-Sat); 12-12:30 Sun
Theakstons XB + guests

This pub is a rock orientated venue in every sense of the word. It is a very friendly place with a live-and-let-live view on life. The exterior is brown glazed tiles, while the interior suffered a pub-co refurbishment a few years ago. A large room is sectioned by pillars and booths, with additional rooms either side of

the main entrance, creating an intimate feel.
🍴🚃(M2)

Sandbar

120-122 Grosvenor Street, M1 7HL
☎ 0161 273 1552   (Map: 17)
🌐 sandbaronline.co.uk
12-12 (1 Thu; 2 Fri-Sat); 12-12 Sun
Joseph Holt Bitter,
Moorhouse's Black Cat +
guests

Situated in the heart of the university area, this is an interesting conversion of old Georgian townhouses attracting custom from both lecturers and students. The atmosphere is bohemian and arty and this is reflected in the excellent beer range both on cask and in bottle (where foreign specialities feature).
Exhibitions of photographs and paintings from local artists usually line the walls while DJs or live music feature in the evenings. The interesting and

varied food menu is available from 12 pm until 7 pm after which a range of proper home-made pizzas are sold until 9 pm. The cider is a changing guest from small producers.

🏵️🍺👜🚃WiFi

Table Table

7-11 Lower Mosley Street, M2 3DW

☎ 0161 702 0974   (Map: 4)

11-11 Mon-Sat; 12-10:30 Sun

Black Sheep Best Bitter,

Golden Sheep

A series of small room-like spaces are sub-divided and predominate the bar serving area, creating a homely environment with modern decor. There is a Costa Coffee café attached to the pub, which serves as the bar for the 200 room Premier Inn next door, though cask ales are not always available.

🏵️👜♿WiFi

Thirsty Scholar

New Wakefield Street, M1 5NP

☎ 0161 236 6071   (Map: 9)

🌐 thirstyscholar.co.uk

Copper Dragon Bitter,

Moorhouse's Bitter

One of the city's first 'arch bars', set under the Oxford Road rail station viaduct. Surprisingly large, it attracts a younger, studenty clientele. It hosts live music on certain nights of the week and the Attic nightclub is upstairs. A cobbled outdoor area adds an interesting element to the pub's cosmopolitan mix. Good quality cask ale is usually prevalent and one beer is rotated on a regular basis. As

you'd expect from its location, it's convenient for trains and many buses pass by.

Please note, at time of going to press, this pub was closed during Network Rail work on viaduct.

🚃(M2)

Other Pubs and Bars in This Area

AXM
121 Princess Street, M1 7AG
☎ 0161 237 0811   (Map: A)
Base Cafe Bar
42 Charles Street, M1 7DB
☎ 0161 273 1011   (Map: B)
Cornerhouse
70 Oxford Street, M1 5NH
☎ 0161 200 1500   (Map: C)
Dokie Dokie Bar
1 Lower Ormond Street, M1 5QF
          (Map: D)
Garratt
127 Princess Street, M1 7AG
☎ 0161 237 5111   (Map: E)
Grand Central
80 Oxford Street, M1 5NH
☎ 0161 236 0890   (Map: F)
Pure Space
11-13 New Wakefield Street, M1 5NP
☎ 0161 236 4899   Map: G)
Retro Bar
78 Sackville Street, M1 3NJ
☎ 0161 274 4892   (Map: H)
Revolution
88-94 Oxford Street, M1 5WH
☎ 0161 236 7470   (Map: I)
Temple
100 Great Bridgewater Street, M1 5JW
☎ 0161 228 9834   (Map: J)
Zouk Tea Bar & Grill
Unit 5 The Quadrangle, Chester Street, M1 5QS
☎ 0161 233 1090   (Map: K)

Oxford Road

Beer Styles

Wide and varied are the beer styles afforded to the modern drinker. The most common and popular ones that may be found around the region are detailed here.

Bitter – Developed towards the end of the 19th century, using the full range of pale and roasted malts, this is the most popular beer style. The hop characters including those of a spicy, peppery and fruity nature may be balanced with juicy and nutty malts and a strong bitterness.

Mild – Usually, it has a colour ranging from the more traditional dark brown with the use of roasted malts, to lighter versions. Typically, it is lower in alcoholic strengths than its counterparts, and is enjoying something of a revival at present.

Old Ale – During the days when beer needed to be stored for a somewhat lengthy period, a long maturation process was used to ensure the beer retained its character. Generally dark in colour, it is not unusual to find lighter versions.

Porter – A beer which gained its popularity with London's market porters in the 18th century, which coined the name and ensured its continued success. It ranges in colour from a dark ruby to an ebony coloured hue, usually with a bitter and fruity taste.

Stout – Previously, this was a variation of a stronger version of the above-mentioned Porter. Originally called Stout Porter, this was introduced to provide a sweeter and less bitter taste.

India Pale Ale (IPA) – Initially brewed for export early in the 19th century to the colonies. They contain a determined hoppy flavour and bitterness, dominated by strong aromas. They can range in colour from a golden tan to a pale bronze.

Pale Ale – A lighter version in its strength and colour than IPA and brewed for the domestic home market. It is dominated by malt and floral flavours, rather than those of a bitter hop.

Golden Ale – Growing in popularity over recent years, especially with the onset of the micro brewery revolution, this is a similar beverage to Pale Ale mentioned above.

Lager - A beer style from Europe which is bottom fermented, and then stored in tanks to mature (known as 'lagering' - lager being German for "to lay down"). It is now becoming increasingly popular with real ale and "craft" brewers, who are reclaiming the style.

Speciality Beer – These can include the likes of various fruits; coriander, liquorice and a mixture of other added flavours give them some strange and wonderful tastes and aromas.

Beer and Cider Festivals

"Ever been to a beer festival?"

"Why would I go to a beer festival - I don't like beer" my friend said.

"Ah, but that is the very reason why you <u>should</u> visit a CAMRA beer festival".

With such a massive variety of real ales available, there is one to suit almost every taste and the perfect place to find the ones to your liking is a beer festival with dozens and sometimes even hundreds of different beers to try under one roof.

Most CAMRA festivals now also include a wide variety of traditional ciders and perries and the larger ones even offer aselection of traditional beer styles from around the world in bottles and / or draught. Its policy at all CAMRA festivals is to give small tasters to the unsure, so you never have to drink something you don't like.

An increasing number of CAMRA festivals serve beer, cider and perry in one third of a pint (in addition to the traditional half and full pint) measures, giving more opportunity to sample the variety on offer and still drink sensibly.

As well as having some of the very best pubs and bars in the country, Greater Manchester can also boast some of the best beer festivals as well. Some are organised solely by CAMRA while others are organised in association with charities or businesses.

Festivals are held throughout the year in all kinds of unlikely locations. See the next page for just some of the CAMRA beer and cider festivals held in and around Manchester every year. There are also an increasing number of pubs and clubs around the country holding their own festivals. Although often smaller than CAMRA festivals, these are well worth checking out as well.

For exact dates, look out for posters, flyers or CAMRA newsletters in local pubs or for a full listing, see the beer festivals section at www.camra.org.uk

The National Winter Ales Festival

Third week in January. Sheridan Suite, Manchester

One of only two CAMRA national festivals. This will be held in Manchester in 2012 and 2013. Host to CAMRA Champion Winter Beer Of Britain Competition. Over 200 real ales, 70+ ciders and extensive foreign and real ale in a bottle bar.

Local CAMRA festivals
*CAMRA in association with other organisations

Bent and Bongs Beer Bash *Atherton and Tyldesley Round Table
Last week in January. Formby Hall, Alder Street, Atherton
Over 100 real ales plus cider and perry bar and draught and bottled foreign beers.

Wigan Beer Festival
First week in March. Robin Park Sports Centre, Loire Drive, Wigan
Over 70 real ales + foreign beers, ciders and perries.

MOSI Real Ale Festival *MOSI
Last weekend in March. Museum Of Science & Industry, Liverpool Road, Manchester.
Relatively new festival in a magnificent location. 50+ real ales all from Greater Manchester breweries, plus cider and perry bar.

Stockport Beer and Cider Festival
Last week in May. Edgeley Park Stadium, Hardcastle Road, Stockport.
The longest established and largest local festival in Manchester

Chorlton Beer and Cider Festival *St Clements Church
Second weekend in July. St Clements Church, Edge Lane, Chorlton.
60+ real ales plus ciders, perries and foreign beers.

Altrincham ABC Festival *Le Trappiste
August Bank Holiday Weekend. Market Hall, Altrincham.
Held in Altrincham's historic covered market hall. 40+ real ales, ciders and perries plus a massive selection of bottled continental beers, many imported specially for the festival.

SIBA Great Northern Beer Festival *SIBA
Last week in October. Ramada Piccadilly Hotel, Portland Street, Manchester.
Society Of Independent Brewers northern beers festival and competition. Over 250 beers from across the north over the week, all on handpumps.

Deansgate-Castlefield

The Rochdale Canal

Deansgate is the main north-south traffic route through Manchester centre. To the north is the recently built Spinningfields district with a mixture of offices, bars & restaurants. The south end of Deansgate borders the popular Castlefield area. The Rochdale and Bridgewater canals meet in Castlefield Basin, surrounded by many old mills that were converted to urban living in the 90s, breathing new life into the area and attracting many bars and restaurants that remain to this day.

Attractions in This Area Include

Deansgate Station
Spinningfields
Museum Of Science & Industry
Opera House
Great Northern Warehouse
Castlefield Basin and Arena
Mamucium Roman Fort

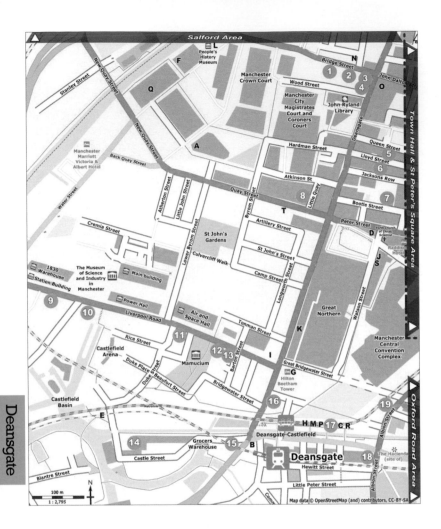

1 Gaslamp
2 B Lounge @ The Bridge
3 Sawyers Arms
4 Lost Dene
5 Rising Sun
6 Old Nags Head
7 Sir Ralph Abercromby
8 Old Grapes
9 Commercial Inn
10 Castlefield Hotel

11 Ox
12 White Lion Hotel
13 Cask Bar
14 Dukes 92
15 Knott Bar
16 Deansgate
17 Pitcher & Piano
18 City Road Inn
19 Britons Protection

B Lounge @ The Bridge

58 Bridge Street, M3 3BW
☎ 0161 834 0242 (Map: 2)
🌐 blounge.co.uk
11-11 (12 Thu; 1 Fri-Sat); 11-11 Sun
Theakston Best Bitter,
Thwaites Bomber + guest

A relatively modest front hides an extremely large pub over two floors. Downstairs is divided into a bar and dining areas, whilst the first floor has a restaurant and a function room. It also gives access to a small, but perfectly formed roof terrace. The bar area is decorated in a mix of traditional and modern; painted brickwork versus wood panels and modern art versus large mirrors. It has a friendly 'front room' feel with bar staff to match. A simple supper is offered on Mondays to Wednesdays after 6.30 pm, with one dish a night. Monday is also iPhone quiz night.
🛏️🕏◑🍴(M1,M2)WiFi

Britons Protection

50 Great Bridgewater Street, M1 5LE
☎ 0161 236 5895 (Map: 19)
11-11; 12-12 Fri-Sat; 12-10:30 Sun
Jennings Cumberland,
Robinsons Unicorn + guests

This Grade II listed 200 year old pub is on CAMRA's National Inventory and the building is bristling with history and character. The long narrow public bar stretches across the width of the front of the building, complete with ornate moulded ceiling. The bar counter and back bar dates

from the 1930s. A hatch in the middle of the back bar serves the two rear rooms accessed via a passageway to the left of the bar. Both rooms have period fireplaces, albeit now gas fired, plus a wealth of other historic features. As well as five cask ales there is an amazing selection of 250 whiskys and bourbons. The pub attracts ale fans, office workers and both concert goers and musicians from the Halle Orchestra who are based at the Bridgewater Hall opposite.
★🛏️🕏◑🍴

Cask Bar

29 Liverpool Road, M3 4NQ
☎ 0161 819 2527 Map: 13)
🌐 caskmanc.co.uk
12-11 Mon-Sat; 12-11 Sun
Up to four guests

Despite its name, this bar specialises in continental beers as well as up to four real ales, with a massive selection both on tap and in bottles. There are no regular cask beers, selections coming from the likes of Abbeydale, Bollington, Hornbeam, Phoenix, Pictish, amongst others are common sights. The pub is small but makes good use of its limited space. An extremely narrow entrance brings you into a small lobby area with the end of the bar on your left and a steep staircase opposite the bar takes you downstairs to the toilets. Beyond the staircase and bar the pub opens out into a larger back room with soft furnishings and a small outside area. Food times and menus are however restricted but you are welcome to bring your own, as long as you take your rubbish with you! ❀➾(M2)WiFi

Castlefield Hotel

Liverpool Road, M3 4JR
☎ 0161 832 7073   (Map:10)
⊕ castlefield-hotel.co.uk
11-11 Mon-Sat; 12-10:30 Sun
Caledonian Deuchars IPA + guests

The lounge bar of this hotel is unusual for a city centre establishment, in that it offers a selection of real ales, the resident one being Caledonian Deuchars IPA, with Copper Dragon Golden Pippin also usually available, plus occasional guests. The decor of the bar is as would expected from a modern hotel; clean and smart, but without the atmosphere of a traditional pub. Quiz night every second and fourth Thursday of the month. The hotel is run by the YMCA and attached to their Y Club gym and sports hall to which guests have access to facilities. The hotel has 48 en-suite bedrooms and extensive conferencing facilities.
Q➾❀⇔◑♣➾(M2)WiFi

City Road Inn

14 Albion Street, M1 5NZ
☎ 0161 236 3820   (Map: 18)
12-11 (1 Fri; 1:30 Sat); 12-10:30 Sun
Black Sheep Best Bitter

The pub dates from 1898 and is situated on a busy corner location close to the Bridgewater Hall and the trendy Deansgate Locks area. From the outside the pub appears to be a typical large inner-city pub, but looks can be deceptive. Inside there are just two rooms, one housing the main bar and another with a pool table. The decor is best described as rustic with bare wooden beams and brewing paraphenalia. The pub is extremely busy on match days when Manchester United are playing at home, with several televisions and drop down screens swinging into action to show the football.
➾❀◑♣➾(M2)

Commercial Inn

125 Liverpool Road, M3 4JN
☎ 0161 834 3504 (Map: 9)
12-11 (11:30 Fri-Sat); 12-10:30 Sun
Joseph Holt Bitter

A traditional street corner local and being located on the edge of the city, is well placed for the Museum of Science & Industry. The area around it has become fashionable in recent times, but the pub remains oblivious to the wine bars and sushi restaurants further along the road with its wall mounted seating, period wallpaper and traditional furnishings. What were once separate rooms to the left and right as you enter have had doors removed and entrances widened to become partitioned areas. The main bar on the right is to the rear of the building with an outside smoking area accessible through a doorway. Budget accommodation is available upstairs.
⌂❀⊯⊟(M2)WiFi

Deansgate

321 Deansgate, M3 4LQ
☎ 0161 839 5215 (Map: 16)
⊕ thedeansgate.co.uk
12-11 (1 Fri-Sat); 12-11 Sun
Thwaites Original + guests

Another of our disappearing traditional street corner locals, sighted within the shadow of Manchester's tallest structure, the Beetham Tower, with an impressive exterior. The interior is no less resplendent, with a certain whiff of old colonialism with its own ambience. From the front bar, there is a stand up drinking area and a delightful array of other rooms and spaces in which to seat yourself. Several mixes of floor coverings and furniture, from church choir stalls, an old settle, some raised areas and lounge seating, borne out of its previous incarnations as the Crown and Galvin's Bar. There is an upstairs function room, which overlooks a stunning roof terrace. A substantial food operation is in evidence and up to four real ales are on offer. Very popular with the 'in' crowd around this busy area of town and can get crowded at times.
⌂➳❀⊍⅃⊟(M2)

Dukes 92

18-20 Castle Street, M3 4LZ
☎ 0161 839 3522 (Map: 14)
⊕ dukes92.com
11:30-11 (1 Fri); 10:30-1 Sat;
10:30-11 Sun
Joseph Holt IPA, Moorhouse's Blonde Witch

This establishment opened in 1991 and is extremely popular in the summer months due to its massive waterside patio area on the Castlefield basin. Inside, the main room on the ground floor has a large open plan area with one side of the L-shaped bar to the right. The most recent expansion has added 'Dukes Grill' restaurant. The upstairs gallery bar is available for hire for private parties along with two other rooms. It began life as a sister bar to Salford's Mark Addy, from which it inherited the legendary cheese and paté selections. Portions are massive; so much so that you should allow plenty of time to eat it, or grab a doggy bag and take some home for later.

Gaslamp

50a Bridge Street, M3 3BW
☎ 0161 478 1234 (Map: 1)
thegaslamp.co.uk
12-11 (12 Thu; 2 Fri-Sat); 12-11 Sun
Up to two guest ales

This is an interesting addition to the city's ever expanding bar scene. Housed in the former Manchester & Salford Children's Mission building, the place has an impressive frontage, but you could easily miss the small doorway that leads down to its basement bar. On descending the dimly lit stairs, the room you enter is certainly different with Victorian glazed brick walls and little in the way of decoration. The bar is along the wall to the rear and is a sparse wooden affair. Tucked away at its end are two handpumps, the real ales on offer bearing no allegiance to 'famous' national brands here; the beers are selected from smaller interesting breweries, many of whom are not seen regularly even in Manchester's multi-ale houses. But they can certainly be one of the most expensive pints of ale in the city.
(M1)WiFi

Knott Bar

374 Deansgate, M3 4LY
☎ 0161 839 9229 (Map: 15)
12-11:30 (12 Thu; 12:30 Fri-Sat); 12-11:30 Sun
Marble Ginger, Manchester Bitter + guests

Nestled in a converted railway arch and opposite the impressive façade of Deansgate rail station, this has been one of the top locals for many years, culminating in being voted Greater Manchester CAMRA Regional Pub Of The Year 2010. It is duly famous for its real ales and extensive range of foreign beers. At least one beer from Marble Brewery is usually present, alongside an ever changing range of beers from local micro breweries and those further afield. Meals are freshly

cooked to order until 8 pm daily, with interesting vegan and vegetarian options available and special requirements are gladly catered for. Decor is simple and unpretentious with sofas and armchairs filling the area by the window facing onto the street, while the external balcony upstairs doubles as the heated smoking area. The bar is centrally located downstairs with the kitchen adjacent and tables and chairs for those drinking and dining opposite.Children are welcome until 8 pm.

⛄🛇◖🚹🐾🚆(M2)

The railway bridges across the roads and canals of the Castlefield area have much elegant ironwork and are also castellated. These ornamental battlements were built as a tribute to the original Roman fort that gave its name to the area.

The Knott is set into a former railway arch and the rumble of the trains overhead is an unusual addition to this bar's facilities.

Lost Dene

144 Deansgate, M3 3EE
☎ 0161 839 9035   (Map: 4)
⊕ thelostdene.co.uk
10-11 (12 Fri; 1 Sat); 10-10:30 Sun

Greene King, Old Speckled Hen, Marstons Pedigree

The former Hog's Head, situated on one of the city's busiest thoroughfares, refurbished and redecorated in the summer of 2011. The decor is not dissimilar to its previous incarnation; the layout retains its centralised bar and wooden polished floor in an ale house style on a mix of levels. Television screens are visible from all directions and there is a Victorian street scene projected from the ceiling, which changes colour. There is a quiz night on Thursdays, private parties can be catered for and there is also a function room upstairs. It can get extremely populated with revellers, especially at weekends and caters for a mixed clientele. To vie with Wetherspoons and the like, there are numerous food promotions with one of the main highlights being the provision of up to four cask ales.

◖🚾🚆(M1,M2)

Old Grapes

Little Quay Street, M3 3JU
☎ 0161 839 4359   (Map: 8)
11-11 (12 Fri-Sat)

Timothy Taylor Landlord, Black Sheep Best Bitter

Nestled in a small street around the corner from the Opera House Theatre, this traditional Victorian looking pub has only recently joined the real ale revolution. Popular with office workers from the nearby Spinnigfields development and theatregoers looking for pre-show dinner and drinks, their busiest time is early evening. All major sports are shown on big screens and local sporting heroes' memorabilia adorn the walls. Food is served 12 pm until 2.30 pm and again from 5 pm until 7 pm. It is closed on Sundays except if football matches are being shown or other events are taking place in the city centre, when food will be available all day. A DJ performs on Friday and Saturday evenings.

☎☕🍴🚻🦽🚆(M1,M2,M3)WiFi

Old Nags Head

19 Jackson's Row, M2 5WD
☎ 0161 832 4315　　(Map: 6)
🌐 old-nags-head.co.uk
11-11:30 Mon-Sat; 11-11:30 Sun
Greene King, Old Speckled Hen + guest

This is a classic Victorian pub interior with plenty of wood panelling and an impressive island bar and staircase. Access from it is attainable from both Jackson's Row and Lloyd Street. The first floor provides a pool room with four pool tables and a function room with a second bar. The second floor has a roof garden, but this is not always open. There is a resident DJ on Friday and Saturday nights with live music on the second Sunday of every month.

🍴🚆🍴🕨♣

Deansgate

Ox

71 Liverpool Road, M3 4NQ
☎ 0161 839 7760　　(Map: 11)
🌐 theox.co.uk
11:30-12 (1 Fri-Sat); 11:30-12 Sun
Black Sheep Best Bitter, Timothy Taylor Landlord + guest

Describing itself as a gastro pub-cum-hotel, 'serving excellent, modern, English food sourced from the finest local ingredients', the pub is food led with the area to the right of the bar reserved for diners. However, drinkers are welcomed in the area of the pub in front of and to the left of the bar. A range of up to five real ales is on offer alongside an extensive wine list. Low level lighting and a traditional rustic decor with solid wooden furniture give the pub a welcoming atmosphere. There is a quiz night every Sunday from 9.30 pm with wine and cash for the winners. The hotel offers accommodation with ten stylish en-suite rooms.

🛏☎☕🚻🍴🦽🚌🚆(M2)WiFi

Pitcher & Piano

Arch 9-10 Deansgate Locks,
Whitworth Street West, M1 5LH
☎ 0161 839 6117 (Map: 17)
⊕ pitcherandpiano.com
12-12 (2 Fri); Sat 11-3; 11-12 Sun
Marstons EPA, seasonal

Situated in the trendy railway arches, this bar provides an unusual option for real ale. The beer choice is from the Marstons range, the bar having two handpumps, with multiple fonts for foreign beers and lagers and there is also a foreign bottled beer selection. The large open plan style bar has three bars on three floors and the lower level has a canalside area which is covered. The interior is contemporary, with comfortable furniture throughout. DJs provide music on Friday and Saturday nights.
🐾◑♿🚌(M2)

Rising Sun

22 Queen Street, M2 5HX
☎ 0161 834 1193 (Map: 5)
11-8; 12-10:40 Tue-Thu; (11:30 Fri-Sat); 1-7 Sun
Timothy Taylor Landlord, Lancaster Blonde + guests

Built in 1684 as a public house this is a little gem and one of only three pubs in the city to have a front and rear entrance. Very popular with local office workers at lunchtimes, the pub welcomes locals and visitors alike. A range of up to five real ales are served from the Lancaster Brewery range, featuring regularly, as do others. Usually closed Monday evenings except when Manchester City or Manchester United football matches are showing on television.
◑🚌(M1,M2)WiFi

Sawyers Arms

138 Deansgate, M3 2RP
☎ 0161 834 2133 (Map: 3)
⊕ orchidpubs.co.uk
12-11 (12 Fri-Sat); 12-10:30 Sun
Moorhouse's Sawyer's Ale + up to three guests

A dramatic looking pub from the outside and boasting that it has held Manchester's longest continuous licence, running from 1734. It has stunning bevelled and engraved glass windows of a bygone era and although much has been altered inside, the bar dominates the main room. Three handpumps are currently available, dispensing regular guests including those from Copper Dragon, Moorhouse's and Northern Blakemere breweries. Food is available from 12 pm until 9 pm each day from a seasonal and modern menu, with a home-cooked style prevailing. There is an upstairs room with a separate bar that can be used for private parties or meetings.
◑♿🚌(M1,M2)WiFi

Sir Ralph Abercromby

35 Bootle Street, M2 5GU

☎ 0161 834 1807 (Map: 7)

Timothy Taylor Landlord,
Copper Dragon Bitter + guest

A traditional back street local, located next door to the city's main police station. Recently redecorated with the emphasis on light colours, polished wood, and all neat and tidy with plenty of drinking space. Catering for the young and older crowds alike, it has a central bar serving all areas of the pub, the former games room now being converted into a function room. The food servery (where Greek food is a speciality) is towards the rear, near the entrance to the beer garden, which spans an L-shaped area, ideal for the summer months.

White Lion Hotel

43 Liverpool Road, M3 4NQ

☎ 0161 832 7373 (Map: 12)

11-11 (12 Fri-Sat); 12-11 Sun

Timothy Taylor Landlord +
guests

A traditional pub modernised to meet the requirements of this newly fashionable end of town and with prices to match. There are two rooms set around a central bar plus an extensive outdoor seating area overlooking the remains of Manchester's Roman fort. The decor reflects a passion for football with Manchester United memorabilia, plus some interesting aerial photos of Manchester in decades past.

🛏🅿🌙🍴♿🚃(M2)WiFi

Other Pubs and Bars in This Area

Alchemist

3 Hardman Street, M3 3HF

☎ 0161 8172950 (Map: A)

Atlas Bar

376 Deansgate, M3 4LY

☎ 0161 834 2124 (Map: B)

Baa Bar

Arch 11 Deansgate Locks, Whitworth St West, M1 5LH

☎ 0161 832 4446 (Map: C)

Bar 38

Peter Street, M2 5GP

☎ 0161 835 3076 (Map: D)

Bohemia

8-9 Catalan Square, Castle Street, M3 4RU

☎ 0161 839 7099 (Map: E)

Cafe Rouge

Leftbank, M3 3AN (Map: F)

Cloud 23 - Hilton Skybar

303 Deansgate, M3 4LQ

☎ 0161 870 1688 (Map: G)

Comedy Store

Arch 3-4 Deansgate Locks, Whitworth Street West, M1 5LH

☎ 0161 839 9595 (Map: H)

Dimitri's

Campfield Arcade, Toneman Street, M3 4FN

☎ 0161 839 3319 (Map: I)

Epernay

1A Watson Street, M3 4EE

☎ 0161 834 8802 (Map: J)

Evuna

277-279 Deansgate, M3 4EW

☎ 0161 819 2752 (Map: K)

Left Bank Cafe Bar
Leftbank, Spinningfields, M3 3ER
☎ 0161 838 9190   (Map: L)
Missoula
Arch 5-6 Deansgate Locks,
Whitworth Street West, M1 5LH
☎ 0161 819 5858   (Map: M)
Mulligans
12 Southgate, M3 2RB
☎ 0161 288 0006   (Map: N)
Pesto Bar
115 Deansgate, M3 2NW
☎ 0161 831 9930   (Map: O)
Revolution
Arch 7 Deansgate Locks,
Whitworth Street West, M1 5LH
☎ 0161 839 7558   (Map: P)
Slug and Lettuce
Left Bank, Irwell Square, Unit 5
Block A, M3 3AN
☎ 0845 1262915   (Map: Q)
Sugar Budda
Arch 12 Deansgate Locks,
Whitworth Street West, M1 5LH
☎ 0161 834 6500   (Map: R)
Taps
1 Watson Street, M3 4EE
☎ 0161 819 5167   (Map: S)
Walkabout
13 Quay Street, M3 3HN
☎ 0161 817 4800   (Map: T)

This publication is a collaboration between the three CAMRA branches that cover Manchester city centre.

North Manchester
Stockport & South Manchester
Trafford & Hulme

Deansgate

Keep up-to-date with the Manchester beers, pubs and bars scene

Opening Times is a large, glossy monthly magazine published by the Stockport & South Manchester branch of CAMRA (the Campaign for Real Ale) and apart from this branch, also covers the surrounding CAMRA branches of North Manchester, Trafford & Hulme, High Peak & North Cheshire, and Macclesfield & East Cheshire. It is free to obtain and available throughout many of the pubs in this guide.

Local Breweries Around the Region

When CAMRA (the Campaign for Real Ale) was formed in 1971, there were less than 200 real ale breweries left in the UK and a worrying trend that threatened to wipe out most of those left. Forty years later we are in the midst of an unprecedented growth in the number of breweries opening, with over 770 breweries now making traditional cask conditioned ale in the UK, more than at any time since the 1940s.

Even countries where there is no real ale tradition like Italy and the USA are seeing new brewers opening up and choosing to cask condition their beers.

Greater Manchester is fortunate in having more of its traditional family brewers surviving than any other area of Britain, with these long established companies happily existing alongside an ever-growing selection of independents ranging from tiny brewpubs to award winning microbreweries of international acclaim.

Over the last 100 years many of Britain's brewing families have sold out to bigger players, so Manchester can be justly proud of having four breweries still owned and run by members of the families that established them.

Between these four alone - Joseph Holt of Cheetham and J W Lees of Middleton to the north of the city, Hydes of Whalley Range on the south side and Robinsons of Stockport - they have over 670 years of brewing pedigree. Even the youngest, Hydes, have been brewing since 1863.

Although between them they own over 700 pubs in Greater Manchester and beyond (400 in the Robinsons family), surprisingly there are only handfuls in the city centre.

The family breweries are the bedrock of Manchester's modern brewing scene. At the other end of the scale, the tiny Bootleg

Brewing Company, based at the Horse & Jockey pub in the suburb of Chorlton was only established in 2010. Almost all their beer flows over the bar of their own pub so the only other place you will see their beers are at the occasional beer festival.

Other Manchester brewpubs include the Star Brewery at the Star Inn, Salford and Greenmill, based at the Cask & Feather pub in Rochdale.

Marble Beers began life in 1998 in the back of the Marble Arch Inn on the northern outskirts of the city centre. Since then beers like

Local Breweries Around the Region

Marble Ginger, Chocolate and Lagonda IPA have become favourites with beer aficionados and regular drinkers alike, with a series of awards from both domestic and international competitions.

As demand for Marble beers grew, in 2009 a larger plant was installed in a unit near the pub, more than doubling their capacity. Marble were outgrowing their brewpub roots and in 2011 the plant at the pub was sold to be the basis of yet another new microbrewery.

Another local microbrewery with an international reputation is Rochdale's Pictish Brewery. Established in 2000 by Richard Sutton, their range of high quality beers, many with distinctive hop flavours, are highly sought after by pubs across the country.

Wigan brewster (a female brewer) Patsy Slevin found fame in 2008 when Oz Clark and James May paid a visit to her Prospect Brewery while filming their Drink to Britain series for BBC2. At the time the brewery was notable for being based in a domestic garage. Successful and popular beers such as Nutty Slack and Silver Tally saw the garage left behind for larger premises and Prospect beers are now available in pubs across the north west.

Dave Porter of Outstanding Beers in Bury not only runs his own successful brewery making award winning beers, he is also

responsible for many breweries across the world. Both Dave's time and the brewery premises are shared with Porter Brewery Installations who can claim to install one in every four new brewery openings in the UK and also run training courses for would be brewers and brewsters.

While Prospect have outgrown their garage for a modern industrial unit, others continue to house themselves in unusual premises. The old mills of the area's industrial heritage are popular locations with recently relocated Shaws Brewery in Stockport, Outstanding of Bury and Greenfield of Saddleworth all taking space in former mill buildings.

Bolton's Bank Top Brewery has set up home in a former tennis club

Local Breweries Around the Region

pavilion - with the first brew in their new home being Pavilion Pale Ale - now one of their flagship beers. Meanwhile, Dunham Massey Brewing Company is housed in the old barn of a farm on the National Trust's Dunham Massey estate.

In a slight twist on the use of old buildings, both Phoenix of Heywood and AllGates of Wigan occupy long abandoned former brewery premises. AllGates are based in what was formerly the brew house for the Dog & Partridge pub while the former Oak Brewing Company moved from Ellesmere Port in 1989, and took both the premises and the name of the original Phoenix brewery that closed in 1937.

While this piece tells you a little about some of our local breweries, there isn't space to mention them all. And even if we did have the space, ultimately breweries aren't about words, they are about beers. The following page lists all of Greater Manchester's breweries (at the time of going to press). While visiting our pubs, keep an eye out for their pumpclips and take the opportunity to sample a local beer in a local pub.

Local Independent Breweries

AllGates (Wigan)

Bank Top (Bolton)

Blackedge (Horwich)

Boggart Hole Clough (Newton Heath)

Bootleg Brewing Co (Chorlton)

Brightside (Bury)

Dunham Massey Brewing Co (Dunham Massey)

Dunscar Bridge (Bolton)

Greenfield (Saddleworth)

Green Mill (Rochdale)

Hornbeam (Denton)

Hydes (Whalley Range)

Joseph Holt (Cheetham)

Irwell Works (Bury)

JW Lees (Middleton)

Leyden (Bury)

Marble (Manchester)

Millstone (Mossley)

Outstanding (Bury)

Phoenix (Heywood)

Pictish (Rochdale)

Prospect (Wigan)

Robinsons (Stockport)

Saddleworth (Saddleworth)

Shaws / Quantum (Stockport)

Star (Salford)

Salford Central

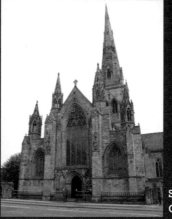

Salford
Cathedral

The area of Salford covered by this guide is the Chapel Street and Crescent corridor through the heart of the old town. It is quite a long and busy stretch of road but produces good results for anyone interested in real ale. The Crescent, built overlooking a bend in the River Irwell, is probably more interesting for the casual visitor as there are two museums and Salford University campus here. Chapel Street is home to the Cathedral, St. Philips Church and Sacred Trinity Church, perhaps a clue to the name. Although overshadowing of the area by adjacent parts of Manchester has seen the decline of its pub stock, Salford Council have ambitious plans for regeneration of the area.

Attractions in This Area Include

Salford Central Station
Salford Crescent Station
People's History Museum
Salford Museum & Art Gallery
Working Class Movement Library
Salford Cathedral

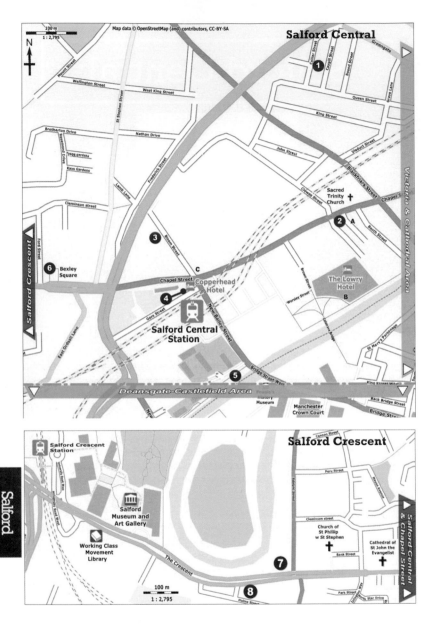

1 Eagle Inn
2 Rovers Return
3 Kings Arms
4 Egerton Arms Hotel
5 Mark Addy
6 New Oxford
7 Old Pint Pot
8 Crescent

Crescent

20 Crescent, M5 4PF
☎ 0161 736 5600 (Map: 8)
⊕ thecrescentsalford.co.uk
12-12 (12:30 Fri-Sat); 12-12 Sun
Up to ten guest ales

This has been a Good Beer Guide regular for many years and the current landlord is maintaining the standard. The twelve handpumps dispense an ever changing range of beers and ciders from all over the place. It is a Grade II listed building as are many of those along this thoroughfare and once said to have been a regular meeting place for Karl Marx and Frederick Engels when it was called the 'Red Dragon'. The pub hosts a regular quiz night on Mondays, open mic night Sundays and the ever popular 'Curry Night', which features on Wednesdays. The interior consists of three oddly shaped rooms surrounding an island bar, with a fourth function -cum-event room to the left hand side and there is a small yard at the rear for when the weather is clement. The pub obtained the area's first 24 hour license, although the facility is rarely used.
🏰🕷🍎🍺

Eagle Inn

18 Collier Street, M3 7DW
☎ 0161 832 4919 (Map: 1)
⊕ joseph-holt.com
12-11 Mon-Sat; 12-11 Sun
Joseph Holt Bitter

This is a hidden gem of a traditional back street boozer and is most commonly known to the locals as the 'Lamp Oil'; you can view the lamp above the entrance door. On entering the pub there are three small rooms off a corridor with a central bar serving traditional ale and the staff and locals make everyone very welcome. It is a Grade II listed building dating from 1902, with a fine terracotta plaque of an eagle with the name above the door and for years this was the only pub sign. Noted as the last only beer house in the area, it is best viewed from the ring road when lit by an autumn or winter sunset; with the red brick and gold lettering illuminated and beckoning you inside, resistance is futile!
♣

Salford

Egerton Arms Hotel

2 Gore Street, M3 5FP
☎ 0161 834 7072   (Map: 4)
11-11 Mon-Sat; 12-7 Sun
Joseph Holt Bitter

From the outside, this looks very much like a Joseph Holt tied house, but is in fact a free house that sells Holt Bitter most of the time. Occasionally a different beer is available, including Holts' seasonal beers or their IPA. This red brick Edwardian two roomed local has generally mature custom and is very handy for Salford central railway station. There is a pool table and television in the vault to the left as you go in. Food is on offer at lunch times in the larger lounge to the right of the bar and some accommodation is available.

ᘒ🍲◖♣

Kings Arms

11 Bloom Street, M3 6AN
☎ 0161 839 8726 or 832 3605
                 (Map: 3)
⊕ studiosalford.com
12-11 (12 Fri-Sat); Closed Sun
Up to six guest ales

This pub was built in 1879 with a semicircular plan at the street corner end and is an impressive Grade II listed red brick building in the gothic style. The original pub was built across the road in 1807, where the former gas offices now stand. It was rebuilt by Cronshaw's Alexandra Brewery, being acquired by Groves and Whitnall in 1899. The pub name is in mosaic above the door and a carved Royal Arms is situated high above this; the corridor by the entrance has a serving hatch on the right (not in use) whilst opposite there is a decent sized snug. After this the main lounge is on the right which is an oval shaped room containing the main bar and another corridor off to the left leads to the beer garden decorated with an eclectic collection of items. The upstairs room is host to film shows and music and is home to Studio Salford - a voluntary art and performance group. The snug also plays host to a popular knitting club on Monday evenings.

Q🍲◖▶

Mark Addy

Stanley Street, M3 5EJ
☎ 0161 832 4080   (Map: 5)
⊕ markaddy.co.uk
11:30-1 (2 Fri-Sat); 11:30-12 Sun
Up to four guest ales

This pub is named after a local hero who saved many people from drowning in the adjacent River Irwell. From the street level entrance and down the stairs which leads into a large lobby, to the left is the riverside terrace and on the right leads into the bar and main room. This is a long lounge with a brick arch ceiling and large plate glass windows which overlook the river. The bar is on

the left hand side as you enter and has four handpumps selling ales from local micro breweries, plus a guest cider. Recently reopened and now specialising in similarly locally produced food is the restaurant, prepared by an award winning chef. There are boat trips run to the Old Trafford football ground on match days.

🏵🍺♿🚪(M3)

New Oxford

11 Bexley Square, M3 6DB
☎ 0161 832 7082 (Map: 6)
🌐 newoxford.co.uk
12-12 Mon-Sat; 12-12 Sun
Up to ten guest ales

This was plainly just the Oxford and formerly owned by Wilsons, then Vaux breweries, a pub which fell on hard times and subsequently closed. Fortunately someone saw potential in refurbishing it, and it reopened in its present format. It is situated on a corner of the street junction across from Salford Magistrates' Court, which itself now has an uncertain future. However, the future of the New Oxford seems secure with its excellent reputation for selling a large selection of real ales from all over the country. Not content with that, real cider is available along with a range of draught and bottled Continental beers. The pub consists of a central bar serving two rooms; the front room is smart with comfy seating with the back room more austere with wooden chairs and tables. Food is available during the day and there are occasional beer festivals drawing large numbers of ale fans, often overspilling into the recently refurbished square.

🏵🍺🍎♿

Old Pint Pot

2 Adelphi Street, M3 6EN
☎ 0161 839 1514 (Map: 7)
🌐 marstonspubcompany.co.uk
11-Late Mon-Fri; 12-Late Sat; 12-Late Sun
Marston's Pedigree,
Wychwood Hobgoblin

Quite a large pub containing a split level and with a long bar downstairs, it is a relatively modern building in contrast to those around it and serves the student community of Salford University. There is an outside terrace with views over the horseshoe bend of the River Irwell which the 'Crescent' is built on. It returned back into the real ale fold in 2010.

🏵🍺♿♣ WiFi

Salford

Rovers Return

89-91 Chapel Street, M3 5DF
☎ 0161 833 2783 (Map: 2)
12-11 Mon-Sat; 12-5 Sun
JW Lees Coronation St

The only pub left on this thoroughfare currently selling cask ale, the pub is a traditional local, housed in a 200 year old building. It serves just the one real ale, therefore establishing its link to its fictional namesake. This one roomed L-shaped pub is deceptively large; the impressive bar has original tiles and woodwork still intact. There are no frills here and although this pub is one of a dying breed the current revitalisation of the Chapel Street area will lead hopefully to a brighter future. Cheap accommodation is available and it may close early if not very busy.

🛏 ♣

Other Pubs and Bars in This Area

Corridor
6-8 Barlow's Croft, M3 5DY
☎ 0161 832 6699 (Map: A)
River Bar (Lowry Hotel)
50 Dearmans Place, Chapel Wharf
☎ 0161 827 4041 (Map: B)
Salford Arms Hotel
146 Chapel Street, M3 6AF
☎ 0161 288 8883 (Map: C)

Beer Academy

beeracademy.org

The beer academy aims to be recognized as a world leader in the provision of education and training in the understanding and appreciation of beer

Salford

Real Cider and Perry

Real cider is a long established traditional drink which is produced naturally from apples and is neither carbonated nor pasteurised. Perry is the equivalent drink made from perry pears and despite what the marketing men would tell you, there is no such thing as 'pear cider'.

Much like real ale, in recent years cider has seen a renaissance in its popularity with drinkers. It is unfortunate that, many of the most well known ciders in the UK are poor imitations of the real thing - cold, carbonated, artificially flavoured liquids that lack the deliciously mellow, aromatic and intoxicating flavours of naturally produced real cider and perry.

Not long after its formation, CAMRA recognised that traditionally made cider and perry was facing a similar threat of extinction to that which faced real ale in the early 1970s and have been supporting producers of the traditional form ever since.

Thankfully, today there are many pubs and bars which offer their customers traditional ciders and perries alongside their real ales. Most commonly these will be found in either a plastic barrel or a box (similar to a wine box) on the back bar, although a number of pubs do dispense traditional cider through a handpump (but beware of non-real ciders such as Addlestones and some Thatchers' brands that are sometimes seen on handpumps).

Look out for the apple symbol ● in the listings to find out which pubs in this guide sell real cider. Beyond the city centre there are many other great cider pubs including the Ye Olde Man & Scythe in Bolton (Greater Manchester's Cider Pub of The Year 2011), the Cheshire Ring in Hyde (Cider Pub of The Year 2010), the Railway at Portwood, Stockport and Ye Olde Woolpack in Edgeley, Stockport.

If you would like to learn more about traditional ciders & perries, visit **camra.org.uk/cider**

Wilmslow Road

The 'Curry Mile', Rusholme

Wilmslow Road is famously Europe's busiest bus corridor thanks to it linking two of Manchester's Universities with the popular residential suburbs of Fallowfield, Withington & Didsbury via the famous "Curry Mile" in Rusholme. Large populations of students and young professionals are served by a vibrant pub scene - this section lists just a few highlights of the many on offer. Buses 42 & 142 amongst many more serve the five miles between Manchester & Didsbury every few minutes.

Attractions in This Area Include

Manchester University
Manchester Metropolitan University
Manchester Museum
Contact Theatre
Whitworth Art Gallery
Whitworth Park
Platt Fields Park
Parrs Wood Entertainment Centre

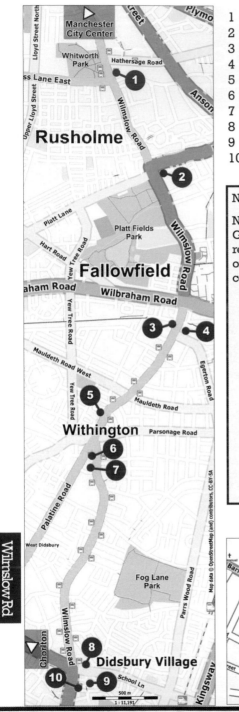

1 Ford Madox Brown
2 Hardy's Well
3 Great Central
4 Friendship
5 Victoria
6 Turnpike
7 Red Lion
8 Milson Rhodes
9 Fletcher Moss
10 Royal Oak

New Good Beer Guide

Now in its 39th edition, CAMRA's Good Beer Guide 2012 is fully revised and updated, with details of more than 4,500 pubs across the country serving the best real ale.

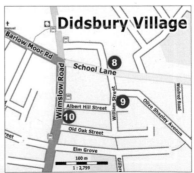

Fletcher Moss

1 William Street, M20 6RQ
☎ 0161 438 0073 (Map: 9)
⊕ hydesbrewery.co.uk
12-11 (12 Fri-Sat); 12-10:30 Sun
Hydes Finest, Original +
seasonals

Named after the alderman who donated the nearby botanical gardens to the city, the atmosphere of this gem is clear even before entering, as the buzz of conversation is audible before opening the door. Inside it is a pub of two halves, with the front encompassing two traditional style snugs, full of Hydes' memorabilia, before opening up into a large bright conservatory area at the rear. However, the convivial atmosphere is maintained throughout by drinkers as mixed in age as they are in their drinking tastes, with real ale, red wine and champagne drinkers alike engaged in lively discourse without having to compete with piped music. The cider cones from the Gwynt y Ddraig producer.
Q❀&●🖾

Ford Madox Brown

Wilmslow Park, Oxford Road, M13 9NG
☎ 0161 256 6660 (Map: 1)
⊕ jdwetherspoon.co.uk
9-12 Mon-Sat; 9-12 Sun
Greene King Abbot Ale,
Ruddles + guests

Built on the site of the old Rusholme Hall this Wetherspoons pub is handy for the University, Curry Mile, Manchester Royal Infirmary and Whitworth Art Gallery. Named after the eminent Victorian Pre-Raphaelite painter whose works hang in Manchester Town Hall and the City Art Gallery (he lived in nearby Victoria Park). Although a modern open-plan pub it has a warmer feeling than you might expect and they go out of their way to build on this with charity and community events. Extra special discounts apply for CAMRA Members on Sunday evenings. Two or three real ciders and perries are also available. Note too that it is open at 8 am for breakfast.
Q❀◑&●🖾

Friendship

351-353 Wilmslow Road, M14 6XS
☎ 0161 224 5758 (Map: 4)
⊕ hydesbrewery.co.uk
12-11 (12 Fri-Sat); 12-11 Sun
Hydes Original, 1863, Finest,
seasonals + guests

Impressive Victorian mansion in a busy student area that attracts a good mix of clientele.

Wilmslow Rd

Refurbished in 2011, the large horseshoe bar serves a variety of areas and can now accommodate 12 cask ales - offering the Hydes range, as well as varying guest beers - ideal for the many festivals the pub hosts. The rear extension completed a few years ago has created the space for provision of interesting and popular Oriental food, including takeaways. Well positioned TV screens provide for sports fans, but to get away from the bustle and hubbub, try the 'Hyde Out' bar in the hut outside for a peaceful drink and a chat. Come the good weather, a variety of outdoor drinking spots are available for people-watching or even bus spotting! Quizzes held weekly with music on Sundays and general knowledge on Tuesdays.

🍴🕮◑🦽🐶🚌

Great Central

306 Wilmslow Road, M14 6NL
☎ 0161 248 1740   (Map: 3)
🌐 jdwetherspoon.co.uk
9-12 Mon-Sat; 9-12 Sun
Greene King Abbot Ale,
Ruddles + guests

Opened in the mid-noughties, this is a Lloyds No 1 bar set beneath apartment accommodation. The name derives from the proximity of the pub to the former railway line that once served the area. A large space has been made to appear more intimate by cleverly breaking the space up with columns, artefacts and good lighting. Although set fair-square in the middle of a student area, this seems to

attract a wide range of customer. That said though, with a number of television screens and a table football machine, it is clear that the company is aiming this venue at a young market whilst retaining their regular Wetherspoon festivals and offers.

🍴🕮◑🦽🐶🚌

Hardy's Well

257 Wilmslow Road, M14 5LN
☎ 0161 257 0450   (Map: 2)
4:30-11 Mon-Sat; 4:30-10:30 Sun
JW Lees Bitter, Sharps Doom
Bar + guests

Formerly the Birch Villa, sited at the southern end of the Curry Mile, noted for its poem writ large on the gable end which dominates the wall overlooking the beer garden (this is by Lemn Sissay, a local poet). Inside this large, high-ceilinged, slightly care-worn,

Wilmslow Rd

one roomed pub there is a cosmopolitan mix of locals and students. Its draught real ales serve as welcome respite to the endless offering of pseudo-Asian lagers from its restaurant neighbours. Evening meals feature steaks, lamb shanks, pizzas, burgers and strangely enough curry! Westons Old Rosie is the cider, and you can find entertainment in the two pool tables and the real Bird of Paradise behind the bar.
⚜🍺♣👜🚃

Milson Rhodes

1d School Lane, M20 6RD
☎ 0161 446 4100   (Map: 8)
🌐 jdwetherspoon.co.uk
9-11:30 (12:30 Fri-Sat); 9-11:30 Sun
Greene King Abbot Ale,
Ruddles + guests

This is Wetherspoon's first venture into Didsbury, named after Dr John Milson Rhodes (1847-1909) who lived in this village, treating patients with learning difficulties and epilepsy. So highly regarded was Dr Rhodes that upon his death Didsbury's tour square clock tower on Wilmslow Road was built to commemorate his life. Beer quality here is assured because the manager drinks cask-conditioned beers herself and uses her own experience and beer preferences to choose which beers to sell. She always tries to mix well-known beers with beers of her own choice, and beers from smaller breweries up and down the country. A micro-brewery Milson Rhodes house-beer is planned for the very near future. Although a modern pub,

a new cask outlet selling up to ten cask conditioned beers with traditional ciders, all sold at very keen prices, is a welcome addition to the Didsbury village pub scene. Look out for regular beer and cider festivals held throughout the year. The pub is also a keen supporter of local charities and regularly raises money for the nearby Christie hospital.
Q⚜🍺♿👜🚃

Red Lion

530-532 Wilmslow Road, M20 4BT
☎ 0161 434 2441   (Map: 7)
🌐 redlionpubmanchester.co.uk
11-11 (11:30 Thu; 12:30 Fri-Sat); 12-11:30 Sun
Jonnings Cumberland,
Marston's Burton Bitter + guests

The oldest pub in Withington (also Grade II listed) and the only one of the three 'Lions' in the village remaining. This 17th century inn appears to be a 'pub for all seasons' with a long, low whitewashed exterior festooned with hanging baskets giving an 'olde worlde' impression immediately contrasting with a 'Free Wi-Fi' sign! The interior presents a similar bewildering contrast,

Wilmslow Rd

central horseshoe-shaped bar displays an impressive collection of old porcelain spirit vats that thankfully were saved from a serious fire in the pub in the 1990s. The pub is famous for its award-winning cheese and pate lunches (served on Mondays to Fridays) which many have tried to copy but none have been able to surpass for choice or value. It can be particularly busy when live sport is screened on television. Four guest beers per month are served.
❀◑🚐

Turnpike

520-522 Wilmslow Road, Withington, M20 4BT
☎ 0161 445 4565   (Map: 6)
11-11 Mon-Fri; 12-10:30 Sun
Samuel Smiths Old Brewery Bitter

Formerly the Wellington, this was acquired when Samuel Smith bought out the Rochdale & Manor brewery. It was extended into the next door shop unit, then renamed in the early '60s. At the same time the interior was thoroughly remodelled with spartan furnishings, a vault to the left with a pebbled chimney breast and the right hand lounge is more comfortably furnished with a Lakeland stone faced fireplace together with wood panelled walls. A recent conversion to cask ale and a listing in CAMRA's National Inventory of Historic Pub Interiors has boosted this pub's profile.
★Q♣🚐

with a low-ceilinged vault area opening up into a larger bar with a more mainstream feel that leads off into a cavernous conservatory. Behind this there is also a magnificent bowling green with extensive outdoor seating around it, making this a very popular pub in summer. There are quiz nights on Mondays, with poker on Thursdays and Sundays, plus Motown nights every second and last Saturdays of the month.
❀◑♿🚐WiFi

Royal Oak

729 Wilmslow Road, M20 6WF
☎ 0161 434 4788   (Map: 10)
11-11 (12 Fri-Sat); 11-11 Sun
Marston's Burton Bitter, Pedigree + seasonal

Built around 1850 this multi-roomed pub is akin to the community centre of the village. It maintains a traditional layout that has served it well over the years. The large

Victoria

438 Wilmslow Road, M20 3BW
☎ 0161 434 2600 (Map: 5)
⊕ hydesbrewery.co.uk
11:30-11 (12 Thu-Sat); 12-11 Sun
Hydes Finest, Original +
seasonals

The period exterior with its etched glass windows hides a l a r g e o p e n - p l a n compartmentalised interior. This area mixes local residents with one of the largest student populations in Europe, who bolster the trade in the evenings. This mix of clientele ensures that the pub is busy at lunchtimes and can be packed in the evenings. The pub also benefits from big screen sports and is an increasingly popular venue for watching the games. It boasts enthusiastic darts teams, alternating live bands and a DJ on Fridays and weekly quiz nights on Thursdays, when competition between students and locals can be boisterous but is always good-natured. At the rear of the pub there is an attractive outdoor beer patio where you can enjoy a cold drink in the sunshine. Recently sensitively refurbished by Hydes, the Victoria now increasingly also sells guest beers and traditional cider. Typically the pub will sell the Hydes' core range together with four or more guest beers, often from micro breweries. The ciders come from Gwynt y Ddraig and Westons and regular promotions include discounted cask beers on Mondays, Thursdays and before 6 pm.

♿ ♣ 👤 🚌

CAMRA and Real Ale

CAMRA (The CAMpaign for Real Ale) came into being in 1971, when four lads, returning from a holiday on the west coast of Ireland decided to form a campaign to promote real ale. Discontented with the keg offerings throughout Britain and the blandness of it all, they decided to do something about it and formed the CAMpaign for the Revitalisation of Ale, as it was originally known.

From a handful of members with cards contained in an old shoe box and working from its beginnings with an address in the suburbs of Salford, Lancashire to its present location in St Albans in leafy Hertfordshire, CAMRA celebrated its 40th birthday in March 2011 and has grown to over 129,000 members and rising. No one could have foreseen or predicted that this would become the biggest consumer campaigning group throughout the kingdom.

What is Real Ale?
The basic ingredients of real ale are malted barley, hops, yeast and water. Yeast ferments the sugars in the malt into alcohol, whilst hops provide a bitter flavour and aroma. Rather than filtering out the yeast, the ale is racked into casks with yeast still present, where a secondary fermentation produces a natural carbonation in the beer and gives the rounded flavours in your glass. The term Real Ale describes the difference between this traditional cask conditioned ale and that of keg beers and lagers that are filtered, pasteurised, chilled and carbonated in the interests of ease of cellaring but losing irreplaceable flavour in the process.

Real Ale in a Bottle
Yes, it is possible to also find real ale in this form, too. The inclusion of added yeast matures the beer in the bottle and often leaves sediment in the bottom. Bottled real ales can be identified by the 'CAMRA says this is REAL ALE' logo, usually found on the label.

Beer Styles
Real ale comes in a variety of styles, every beer having its own unique flavour, aroma, strength and colour. The best way of appreciating them and finding out what suits you best, is to try them all! (But not all at once though, we hasten to add, as CAMRA promotes responsible drinking).

Beer strengths are given in percentages of abv's (alcohol by volume) and for a more detailed description, please see our separate article on *Beer Styles*.

Chorlton-cum-Hardy

Old Tramways Offices, Barlow Moor Road

This once anonymous suburb of Manchester has in recent years become the city's most vibrant suburb with a plethora of new modern bars opening alongside more established pubs. Such is the variety on offer that it has become a destination in itself for fans of cask ales. The area has excellent public transport links from central Manchester via the frequent buses (numbers 84, 85 & 86 from Piccadilly Gardens) and the Metrolink tram system's South Manchester line.

Attractions in This Area Include

**Chorlton Ees Nature Reserve
Chorlton Park
Manchester Southern Cemetery
Chorlton Water Park**

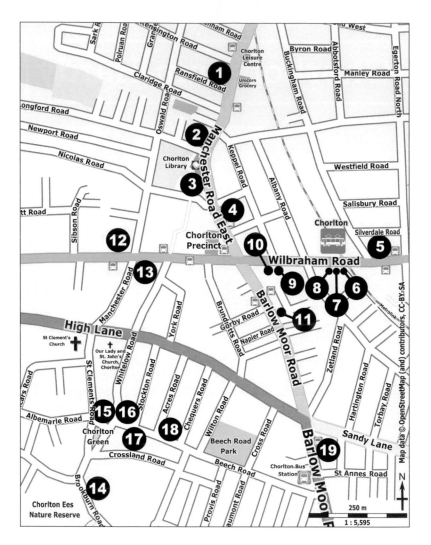

1 Pi	11 Duffy's Bar
2 Marble Beer House	12 Spread Eagle
3 Sedge Lynn	13 New Lloyds Hotel
4 Charango	14 Bowling Green
5 Oddest	15 Horse & Jockey
6 Bar	16 Beech Inn
7 Nook	17 Famous Trevor Arms
8 Gallery	18 Parlour
9 Electrik	19 Escape
10 Dulcimer	

ROBINSONS BREWERY   OFFICIAL SPONSOR

Bar

533 Wilbraham Road, M21 0UE
☎ 0161 861 7576   (Map: 6)
12-11:30 (12 Thu; 12:30 Fri)
11.30-12.30 Sat; 11:30-11:30 Sun
Marble Ginger, Manchester Bitter + guests

The first of this area's modern café bars created in the late '90s and still going strong 15 years later. The emphasis is on real ale and good quality food with meals being served until 9 pm each evening and Sunday lunches are extremely popular. Its seven handpumps are tucked away on the section of the bar farthest from the door. Two beers are usually available from the Marble brewery range, alongside up to five guest beers with the emphasis being on local breweries. Well behaved children are welcome until 8pm.

꧁❀◖♣WiFi

Beech Inn

72 Beech Road, M21 9EG
☎ 0161 881 1180   (Map: 16)
5-11 (12 Fri); 12-12 Sat; 12-11 Sun
Timothy Taylor Landlord, Golden Best, Copper Dragon Golden Pippin + guests

A multi roomed local which has retained its traditional layout

and pleasant décor, where the bay windowed front bar room looks out over the village green and the rear bar room contains a dartboard and a piano. To the right of the entrance is the snug, a popular spot for the local musicians who gather for jam sessions, including folk and Cajun nights. This pub lies very much at the heart of the local community and visitors seeking out its cask ales and traditional atmosphere are most welcome. There is outdoor seating to the front and also in the enclosed rear yard, with well behaved children welcome until 7 pm.

ꦂQ꧁❀♣

Bowling Green

Brookburn Road, M21 9ES
☎ 0161 860 2800   (Map: 14)
12-11 (12 Fri-Sat); 12-11 Sun
Greene King Old Speckled Hen, Timothy Taylor Landlord

This is a large pub which sits comfortably across the village green, priding itself on its community links and is popular for sports, particularly football, rugby and GAA Gaelic football. Food is served on Mondays to Fridays from 12 pm until 7.30 pm and on Saturdays and Sundays from 12 pm until 7 pm. There are quiz nights every Thursday from 9 pm and a disco

every Sunday night.
Q ⛺ 🐾 ◐ ♿ ♣ WiFi

Charango

456a Barlow Moor Road, M21 0BQ
☎ 0161 881 8596   (Map: 4)
🌐 charango-chorlton.co.uk
5-12 (1 Fri); 10-1 Sat; 10-12 Sun
Thwaites Wainwright + guest

A themed tapas bar specialising in a range of freshly prepared dishes from South America, all reasonably priced with special offers available. On the drinks front there are up to two or three traditional British ales which can be ordered at the bar or served at tables. There are DJs playing and on some occasions live musicians playing Latin music at weekends.
🐾 🐾 ◐ ♿ WiFi

Duffy's Bar

398 Barlow Moor Road, M21 8AD
☎ 0161 881 6789   (Map: 11)
2-11; 12-12 Fri-Sat; 12-11 Sun
JW Lees Bitter, Black Sheep Best Bitter + seasonal

A small corner bar just south of the main centre, where the focus is definitely on sport, with the bar at its busiest for the showing of GAA Gaelic football, but also accommodates Premiership football, golf and horse racing fans, etc. The sporting theme continues with walls decorated with selections of sporting memorabilia, with no particular allegiance shown; items from Manchester City and Manchester United football clubs having equal prominence, also rugby and GAA shirts with a wealth of

photographs. On most Saturdays and some Sundays from 8 pm there is free entry to the live music sessions.
🐾

Dulcimer

567 Wilbraham Road, M21 0AE
☎ 0161 860 0044   (Map: 10)
🌐 dulcimer-chorlton.co.uk
4-12:30 (1.30 Fri); 12-1.30 Sat;
12-12:30 Sun
Outstanding Blonde On Blonde, Thwaites Wainwright + guests

This is one of the most popular of the café bars in this area, set on two levels with an enclosed drinking yard to the rear. The décor is stripped back and basic, with the walls of bare brick and varnished floors and an array of antique and reclaimed furniture. Regular live music is held in the upstairs bar which features a mixture of established and new acts with the emphasis on singer songwriters, whilst DJs play music at the weekends. There is a limited food menu of simple snacks with the cheese and paté platters being their most popular dish.

🕹🎶🕹🎶

Electrik

559 Wilbraham Road, M21 0AE
☎ 0161 881 3315   (Map: 9)
🌐 electrikbar.co.uk
1-12; 12-12 Tue-Thu (1 Fri-Sat); 12-12 Sun

Thwaites Wainwright + guests

This is a 'part café, part pub' by day and a modern bar by night with friendly service and a varied drinks menu. It attracts people of all ages, who have made this simple operation well known across the area and seen it nominated for numerous awards. From young mums with coffee and cake to the cocktail drinking twenty somethings and senior citizens enjoying the regular changing range of cask ales, all walks of life are welcome here. Weekend evenings can be busy with the younger element that is attracted to the music from the free jukebox or the DJs, and the clientele remains mixed. Foodies are well catered for too, with simple meals and snacks all being available until 9 pm.

🛏🕹🎶🕹🎶WiFi

Escape

370 Barlow Moor Road, M21 8AZ
☎ 0161 862 9911   (Map: 19)
3-11; 12-12 Fri-Sat;12-11 Sun

Up to two guest ales

A friendly little bar sitting opposite the bus station, which is small fronted but deep once

within. Its location away from the hustle and bustle of the area's main thoroughfare leaves it with a more down to earth atmosphere than the nearby Beech Road stretch of bars and it can be a pleasant stop for a quiet daytime drink. There are 'open mic' nights hosted along with a variety of DJs throughout the week.

🛏🕹🎶WiFi

Famous Trevor Arms

135 Beech Road, M21 9EQ
☎ 0161 881 8209   (Map: 17)

Timothy Taylor Landlord + guests

This is a traditional pub which retains its separate lounge and areas, each served by a common bar. The lounge is host to karaoke and discos at weekends, while the bar to the left is more peaceful. One of the few pubs in the area to show live football matches, hence both rooms can get busy during these transmissions. There is an enclosed yard to the rear.

🕹

Gallery

537-539 Wilbraham Road, M21 0UE
(Map: 8)
12-11 (11:30 Wed-Thu; 1:30 Fri-Sat); 12-11:30 Sun

Hydes seasonal + guests

A large establishment, this was

formerly named Abode and is best known for its regular live music and DJs, attracting a somewhat younger clientele than some of the other bars around this area. It does have a more sedate side to it though, when the bar has its quieter moments. Televised football matches are shown regularly.

Horse & Jockey

9 Chorlton Green, M21 9HS
☎ 0161 860 7794   (Map: 15)
⊕ horseandjockeychorlton.com
12-11 (11:30 Thu; 12 Fri-Sat); 12
-11 Sun

Bootleg Brewing Co beers, + guests

This is a historic old hostelry facing the village green and totally rejuvenated under its new ownership since 2009. It is now home to the Bootleg brewing company, plus won the Kennel Club 'Open For Dogs' award in 2010 with a bottled non-alcoholic dog beer available. It has up to six cask ales with usually at least one from their pub's brewery. Food is available everyday until 10 pm (8 pm on Sundays) with vegan, vegetarian and gluten free options and there is a restaurant upstairs open

evenings and weekends. Beer festivals are held twice a year, a farmer's market and craft fair on the last Saturday of the month, and an acoustic night on the second Wednesday, with a quiz night on Sundays.
WiFi

Marble Beer House

57 Manchester Road, M21 9PW
☎ 0161 8819206   (Map: 2)
12-11 (11:30 Thu; 12 Fri-Sat); 12
-11:30 Sun

Marble Ginger, Manchester Bitter + guests

A stalwart of the bar scene in this area, it is a Mecca for cask ale lovers and serves a rotating and varied range of beers from the Marble brewery. It also stocks a number of guest ales from local breweries plus a good choice of bottled beers, including Marble and a range of others. Real cider has a

THE BOOTLEG
★ EST. 2010 ★
BREWING COMPANY

CHORLTON'S BOUTIQUE BREWERY
Beers available at the Horse & Jockey and selected festivals

Bootleg Brewing Co, The Green, Chorlton
0161 860 7794 info@horseandjockeychorlton.com
horseandjockeychorlton.com/microbrewery

presence too, the current ones displayed on a chalkboard and dispensed from a jug kept in the fridge. A welcoming atmosphere and interested staff create a relaxed place to meet with friends, read the many books or bring your dog (if you have one) to sit by your side.
Q ☕ 🐕 & 🍎

New Lloyds Hotel

Wilbraham Road, M21 9AN
☎ 0161 286 0693   (Map: 13)
12-11:30 (12 Fri-Sat); 12-12 Sun
JW Lees Bitter + seasonal

This is a large, beautiful late Victorian listed building, built in 1900 and balances traditional style with modern tastes. Up to four cask ales are available and it offers food daily, freshly made and sourced from local ingredients. A wide range of televised sporting events are shown on multiple screens, and the bowling club plays on their purpose built green outside. There is also an outdoor patio to the side and tables by the pavement at the front which provide additional seating. Regular live music performances are featured on four nights of the week.
♨ ☕ 🐕 ◐ & ♣

Nook

535 Wilbraham Road, M21 0UE
☎ 0161 8820700   (Map: 7)
1-11:30 (12 Wed-Thu; 12:30 Fri-Sat); 1-12 Sun
Wells & Youngs seasonal + guest

A just name for this tiny nook of a bar nestled between its larger neighbouring ones. It has a

quirky feel, which attracts a bohemian crowd. There are two handpumps serving guest ales, with real ciders and perries sitting on the back bar. The selection of draught and bottled world ales is impressive and extensive, as is their range of spirits which feature 11 single malt whiskeys, 13 different varieties of rum and numerous varieties of gin, tequila, sambuca and many more are also prevalent. Evenings feature DJs on many nights with a varied range of music which can include reggae, hip hop and Latin nights.
☕ 🐕 ◐ ♣ 🍎 WiFi

Oddest

414-416 Wilbraham Road, M21 0SD
☎ 0161 860 7515   (Map: 5)
🌐 oddbar.co.uk
5-11:30; 11-11:30 Tue-Thu (1:30 Fri); 10-1:30 Sat; 10-11:30 Sun
Northern Oddest Ale + guests

The newest addition to this ever popular group of bars which also includes Odd and Odder. Like its siblings the decor is distinctly eclectic with a collection of Turkish lamps in one corner and a wall of cassette tapes in another setting the tone. A range of six ever changing real ales favouring local breweries also includes real cider and perry, whilst

breweries large and small, near and far. The staff appear attentive, friendly and relaxed, with the accent on customer focus. The food offering is classic British including dishes such as faggots with mash and gravy, hunters pie and Lancashire hot pot. There are separate breakfast, lunch and dinner menus so what is available depends on the time of day.

🦴🕷🍺

Albany Road, Chorlton, was for many years the home of Cosgrove Hall, the famous children's' TV production company. It has produced the likes of Danger Mouse, Chorlton and the Wheelies, Postman Pat and Count Duckula. Parallel to Albany Road is Keppel Road, childhood home of the Bee Gees

there are selected world beers dispensed on draught and in bottles. A free jukebox is stocked up by the independent Kingbee Records and on Wednesday nights there is 'Quizimodo', the quiz with a difference. Food is served until 9 pm daily, with Sunday roasts being popular. Children are welcome until 7 pm each evening, with their own special food menus and film afternoons.

🦴🕷🍺🐶 WiFi

Parlour
60 Beech Road, M21 9EG
☎ 0161 881 4871 (Map: 18)
🌐 parlour.info
12-11 (1 Fri); 10-1 Sat; 10-11 Sun
Timothy Taylor Landlord + guests

A small, modern bar serving quality food and drink, where the left hand section tends towards the diners, including table service, but still with plenty of room for drinkers in the bar area. Up to six cask ales are available from a variety of

Pi
99 Manchester Road, M21 9GA
☎ 0161 882 0000 (Map: 1)
🌐 pi-chorlton.co.uk
11-11 Mon-Tue (12 Wed-Thu; 12:30 Fri); 12-12:30 Sat; 12-11 Sun
Tatton Blonde + guests

A small bar and Manchester's original craft beer bar serving only quality UK and Continental beers sold from its four handpumps (including a real cider). Alongside the real ales sit a selection of nine draught lagers and beers from far and wide. Amongst all these are the bottled varieties; no less than 80 from around the world which can be selected from the menus placed on every table. With friendly and helpful staff, there

are nice touches like complimentary peanuts offered with every purchase. As implied by its name, as well as the amazing range of beers, it also does a roaring trade in pies with gourmet offerings from the Pieminister food company with a choice of mash, peas and gravy, and food is available until 11 pm each evening.

🛏🕸🍽🍴 WiFi

Sedge Lynn
21a Manchester Road, M21 9PN
☎ 0161 860 0141   (Map: 3)
🌐 jdwetherspoon.co.uk
8-11 (12 Fri-Sat); 8-11 Sun
Greene King Abbot Ale,
Ruddles + guests

A J D Wetherspoon pub converted from a former Temperance Movement billiard hall housed in an unusual building with its high barreled ceiling and the space below which cleverly breaks up the room. As with all their pubs,

meals are served at breakfast times (8 am until 12 pm) and the main menu at all times up to 10 pm at night. A keen supporter of local breweries, generally there are up to six real ales on at any time, including real cider. The clientele is varied and eclectic across the age range, which makes this an interesting place to drink.

Q🛏🕸🍽🍴 WiFi

Spread Eagle
526-528 Wilbraham Road, M21 9LD
☎ 0161 861 0385   (Map: 12)
🌐 joseph-holt.com
Joseph Holt Bitter, Mild

Around 10 years old, it is very much a 'traditional' pub in the Joseph Holt style. A pool table sits in the main lounge bar and there are televisions as the pub is popular for sporting events, and there are DJs or karaoke at the weekends. To the rear is a smaller bar with darts and other pub games and the novel option of 'big screen' Nintendo Wii. Children are welcome during the day, but the pub operates an over 21s policy in the evenings and on Thursdays there is a quiz night from 9 pm. Accommodation is also available at bargain rates for this part of the town.

🕸🍴🍀

Index of Pubs Serving Real Ale